NORM AND ORDER

NORM AND ORDER

An investigation into logic, semantics,
and the theory of law and morals

by

JOVAN BRKIĆ

Professor of Philosophy
North Dakota State University

HUMANITIES PRESS
NEW YORK

Printed in the United States of America

To Beverly, Vida, and Alexandra

FOREWORD

The work set forth here has germinated over a period of years in response to immense methodological and theoretical problems which we encountered while conducting empirical investigations into law and morals. We looked then in vain for a work that could delineate the issues and offer more than a reliance on intuitive stereotypes of jurisprudence and descriptive ethics. The relevance of contemporary logic and semantics to descriptive and theoretical ethics became clearer and clearer to us as we proceeded in our investigations. We hope to have demonstrated this relevance in our work, but we hope even more that the relevance of the theory of law and morals to jurisprudence and descriptive ethics comes clearly through in our work, as well as the relevance of descriptive ethics and jurisprudence to theoretical ethics and philosophy of law.

ACKNOWLEDGMENTS

Our debts are many. Dean Seth Russell, the wisest and kindest dean, made possible the execution of this work. Dean Glenn S. Smith encouraged and supported it. To Willard Van Orman Quine, Hans Kelsen, Nicolai Hartmann, and Hermann Wein we are indebted intellectually; to the former two through their works, and the latter two as teachers.

My friend Charles King, Professor of Sociology at North Carolina College, read the whole manuscript and commented on it. Joseph M. Bochenski, Professor of Philosophy at the University of Fribourg, read the first part of the work, commented on it and encouraged its publication.

Hector-Neri Castañeda, Professor of Philosophy at Wayne State University; Carl Wellman, Professor of Philosophy at Washington University; Layman E. Allen, Associate Professor of Law at Yale Law School; William Query, Chief of Psychological Services at the Veterans Administration Hospital in Fargo, North Dakota; Joy Query, Associate Professor of Sociology at North Dakota State University, and Antony Oldknow, Assistant Professor of English at North Dakota State University, all read portions of the manuscript and commented on them.

We owe to Catherine Cater and Delsie Holmquist, professors of English at North Dakota State University, a discussion on the interpretation of the imperative usages of 'shall'.

Mrs. Beverly Brkić, Head of the Catalogue Department at North Dakota State University Library and my wife, cleaned the manuscript stylistically.

Mrs. Mary Yirchott and Mrs. Helena Wilcox rendered all the secretarial assistance.

Our gratitude goes to all of them for their services.

J. B.

CONTENTS

PHILOSOPHICAL ANALYSIS OF NORMATIVE DISCOURSE

THEORY OF LAW AND MORALS

NORM AND ORDER

PHILOSOPHICAL ANALYSIS
OF NORMATIVE DISCOURSE

PHILOSOPHICAL ANALYSIS AND NORMATIVE DISCOURSE

I. *Law and Morals*

The philosophical analysis of normative discourse must assume as an empirical fact, first, the existence of normative discourse, and second, that normative discourse is the means by which normative contents are expressed. 'Normative contents' is the term that will be used to stand for moral and legal values, ideals, ideas, norms, principles, and commands. A customary, although not a clear, distinction is made between legal values, ideals, ideas, norms, principles, and commands on the one hand, and moral, sometimes also called ethical, ones on the other hand. When such a distinction is made, the term 'law' is used to stand for the former, and the term 'morals,' sometimes also called 'ethics,' for the latter.

No universally acceptable definition of either law or morals has been made and it is doubtful if one ever will be proposed. But even though this is the case, working definitions can be advanced and are desirable, if for no other reason than to indicate the presuppositions that lurk behind every normative analysis. For present purposes, therefore, let law and morals be defined as the *primary* instruments of social control. The qualification *primary* is added to indicate that alternative means of social control, such as sheer force, conditioning, and economic pressure, are at least theoretically possible, and indeed are used in connection with law and morals. Other definitions, perhaps more extensively elaborated, could be adduced.[1] The purpose of this one, however, is to chart the road, not to explicate.

If law and morals are primary instruments of social control, the question at once arises, what is the relationship between them? This is one of the most difficult questions to answer satisfactorily, for

---

[1]Cf. H. Kantorowicz, *The Definition of Law* (Cambridge: Cambridge University Press, 1958), p. 21; and H. M. Kallen, "Morals," *Encyclopaedia of the Social Sciences*, X, 643, for alternative possibilities.

Not only law and morals share a vocabulary so that there are both legal and moral obligations, duties, and rights; but all municipal legal systems reproduce the substance of certain fundamental moral requirements. Killing and the wanton use of violence are only the most obvious examples of the coincidence between the prohibitions of law and morals. Further, there is one idea, that of justice, which seems to unite both fields; it is both a virtue specially appropriate to law and the most legal of virtues.[2]

The problem becomes complicated if non-Western societies such as tribal or Islamic societies, which neither draw nor admit a distinction between law and morals, are taken into account. And even in the West the problem becomes quite complicated by considering law and morals, quite properly, in connection with social ideals, political views, and religious beliefs. Moreover, that which is generally considered to be a matter of morals and that which is a matter of law varies even in the West from one nation to another, or even within one nation at different times. There is no essential difference between the two.[3] Nor is there any difference between them so far as the language used to express them is concerned. But this functional and empirical distinction in the present world can be established: law is the primary instrument of social control which utilizes organized force to enforce external compliance with its prescriptions (exclusive of international law);[4] morals do not ordinarily use organized force to impose their prescriptions, but rather psychological and social pressure.

---

[2]H. L. A. Hart, *The Concept of Law* (Oxford: The Clarendon Press, 1961), p. 7.

[3]A different view is taken on this issue by Hans Kelsen, *Reine Rechtslehre* (Leipzig: Frank Deuticke, 1934), pp. 12ff. However, Kelsen does not claim empirical evidence in support of his view, but rather considers his view as a desideratum of "pure law."

[4]Cf. also Hart, p. 25.

II. *Language*[5]

1. It is impossible at present to offer a total definition of *language* that will be fully justified from the standpoints of general linguistics, semantics, and logic, the sciences that deal with *language;* let alone to arrive at a definition that will be satisfactory to everyone. What can be done, however, is to offer a working definition of *language* for the purposes at hand: *Language* is the term that applies to a class of human means for communicating information, feelings, attitudes and experiences.[6] The subclasses of *language* are: natural language families such as Indo-European, Finno-Ugric, etc.; the class of artificial or formalized languages such as the languages of symbolic logic; and the mixed class of natural and artificial languages.[7]

Artificial or formalized languages are constructed for certain restricted and specialized purposes. They consist of strings of signs connected by the rules of juxtaposition, and by their very design are intended to be 'fixed,' not subject to development in time, and are devoid of feelings, attitudes, or human experience. They represent timeless models constructed for their own sake, although they may have a variety of applications, one of them being the formal analysis of natural languages. The use of artificial languages for the purpose of formal analysis of natural languages can be of considerable importance for the study of law and morals.

The natural or ordinary languages are the only subclass of *language* that are used to communicate the whole range of information, feelings, attitudes, and human experience. No natural language

---

[5]Significant portions of the ensuing sections of this essay represent a paper that was read and criticized by Profs. Layman Allen of Yale Law School, Hector-Neri Castañeda of the Philosophy Department, Wayne State University, Carl Wellman of the Philosophy Department, Lawrence University, and Antony Oldknow of the English Department, North Dakota State University. A drastically revised version of that paper is incorporated in this essay. The criticisms of Professors Allen and Castañeda were of a general nature, while those of Professors Wellman and Oldknow were both general and specific. Special acknowledgments, in addition to this general one, will be given in appropriate places where suggestions of the critics were accepted.

[6]Carl Wellman's objection that this definition is too narrow since it does not take care of performative utterances and critical language can be met by the explication that the terms 'attitudes' and 'feelings' are broad enough to incorporate performative utterances such as 'I promise,' as well as what Wellman called 'critical language' in *The Language of Ethics* (Cambridge: Harvard University Press, 1961).

[7]I owe a debt here to Professor Oldknow.

is completely divested of any of these. Hence, no natural language
is used to communicate *only* information, or feelings, or attitudes,
or experience, although any one of these features can be stressed
over the others. Thus, for example, the informative aspect of natural languages is stressed in expository prose, or the emotional color
in poetry.

A fluent native speaker acquires 'understanding' of his language through the experience of listening to it and speaking it, and
by means of 'intuition' and 'feeling.' The intuitive understanding of
a natural language is never completely precise. Hence it is oftentimes inadequate for scientific purposes, many times inadequate for
the purposes of law and morals, and sometimes inadequate even
for the purposes of everyday life. The inability of a fluent native
speaker to grasp completely his language extends from individual
words to the whole context of his native language.

'Analysis' is a complementary means that can be used for "understanding" natural language. Analysis, however, even when it is
applicable, cannot replace intuition, but merely supplement it. The
analytic methods thus far developed cannot yield a complete, but
only a partial, analysis of the given natural language.[8] There are no
purely analytic and formal methods which would make it possible
to decide whether a given discourse is coherent or incoherent. The
only way to 'know' whether a given discourse is or is not coherent
is by intuition. No known analytic methods can thus extend to the
discourse, let alone to the whole natural language. This fact leads
to the conclusion that 'intuitive understanding' will have to remain
as a crucial criterion in understanding the natural language as such,
with analytic and formal methods to be used whenever possible to
clarify and occasionally to correct what is 'understood' intuitively.

2. Every natural language, and hence every language of the
given normative system, has a structure of its own that is open to
grammatical analysis. The number of grammatical elements in a
natural language is restricted, and therefore a complete grammatical

---

[8]Known analytic methods can be applied for a partial analysis of words and
sentences, and in the case of logical analysis even to a string of sentences, but not
beyond.

One of the few attempts at discourse analysis so far has been made by Zellig
S. Harris, "Discourse Analysis," reprinted in *The Structure of Language: Readings
in the Philosophy of Language*, ed. J. A. Fodor and J. J. Katz (Englewood Cliffs:
Prentice Hall, 1965), pp. 355-389. It cannot be said that this attempt was successful.

analysis of a natural language is in principle possible.[9] This fact has the important consequence that no matter what the intuitive grasp of the grammatical structure of the given language is, it can be verified by analysis.

The fundamental material components of natural language are the units of phonology, graphology, gesticulation, and derived, secondary systems. These expound the elementary meaning units, or morphemes,[10] which represent the semantic level. On the semantic level speech consists in the selection of elementary linguistic units and their combination into complex units according to the syntactical rules of the respective language. Thus are formed sentences, utterances, and finally discourse. The speaker must choose words that are a part of the linguistic store held in common by him and his listeners, and in addition he must observe the syntactical and logical rules in order to be understood.[11] But:

> Within these limitations we are free to set words in new contexts. Of course, this freedom is relative, and the pressure of current clichés upon our choice of combinations is considerable. But the freedom to compose quite new contexts is undeniable, despite the relatively low statistical probability of their occurrence.
>
> Thus in the combination of linguistic units there is an ascending scale of freedom. In the combination of distinctive features into phonemes, the freedom of the individual speaker is zero; the code has already established all the possibilities which may be utilized in the given language. Freedom to combine phonemes into words is circumscribed, it is limited to the marginal situation of word-coinage. In the forming of sentence out of words the speaker is less constrained. And finally, in the combination of sentences into utterances, the action of compulsory syntactical rules ceases and the freedom of any individual speaker to create novel contexts increases sub-

---

[9]Cf. Roman Jakobson, "Typological Studies and their Contribution to Historical Comparative Linguistics," *Selected Writings* ('S-Gravenhage: Mouton and Co., 1962), I, 530.

[10]I am indebted here to Professor Oldknow. Cf. also Roman Jakobson and Morris Halle, *Fundamentals of Language* ('S-Gravenhage: Mouton and Co., 1956), pp. 3f.

[11]*Ibid.*, pp. 58ff.

stantially, although again the numerous stereotyped utterances are not to be overlooked.[12]

It is significant to note that the freedom of selection of units
and their combinations increases as we advance from the phonol-
ogical to the semantic level, the level of language in which we are
particularly interested. It should also be noted that the science of
linguistics has not yet been able to cope with the emotive and ex-
pressive aspects of natural language beyond barely acknowledging
the fact of their existence.[13] Nor has the science of linguistics managed to go beyond the analysis of sentences to other elements of
discourse.[14] Hence the linguistic analysis of natural language
amounts to the analysis of sentences and their components. And even
so this analysis can at best be only partial, since it cannot be applied
to emotive contents nor the sociocultural context, both of which
loom large in the language of law and morals.

III. *Normative Discourse*

1. Normative contents are communicable only if they can be
expressed in some language. Such a language can in principle be an
artificial or a natural language. It is an empirical fact that normative
contents have always been expressed by means of natural language;[15]
oftentimes the same normative contents have been expressed in a
number of natural languages. Indeed, with some restrictions, any
natural language can be used to express historically known normative contents. We shall proceed on the assumption that normative
contents will be expressed in the future likewise by means of natural language.

2. Syntactic rules of natural language allow the formation of
an infinite number of sentences. It is an empirical fact, however,
that only a finite number of sentences will be formed in a given
natural language. On either count the basic syntactic unit of natural

---

[12]*Ibid.*, p. 59.

[13]*Ibid.*, p. 9; also Bertil Malmberg, *Structural Linguistics and Human Communication* (New York: Academic Press, 1963), pp. 18ff.

[14]As noted above, one of the few attempts to accomplish this was made by
Harris.

[15]Traffic lights and similar devices, which could count as artificial language,
do not contradict this statement since they are used simply as abbreviations for
traffic regulations expressed in full by means of natural language.

language is *sentence*. Since natural language can be represented as an infinite or finite disjunction of conjunctions,[16] with negated or unnegated components, depending on whether empirical facts of language are taken into consideration or not, the solution of the problem of analysis of language will consist in the general solution of the problem of sentence analysis.

3. An exhaustive analysis of sentences in all the natural languages is neither possible nor necessary. It is impossible since an infinite number of them can be generated. It is unnecessary since sentences of one natural language, with some restrictions, have their analogues in other natural languages, and the methods developed for the analysis of sentences in one natural language can be extended to other natural languages. Moreover, even the analysis of all the sentences in one natural language is neither possible nor necessary. It is impossible since again there are an infinite number of sentences that can be formed in a given natural language;[17] and it is unnecessary since there are a finite number of basic types in any natural language through which normative contents can be expressed.

4. Normative contents are usually organized, more or less loosely, in a system which is expressed by means of natural language. A normative system may consist of a number of items such as a code of law; a moral code; judicial decisions; jurisprudential, casuistic, and similar items.[18] Traditionally four basic types of sentences are isolates of such a system: (a) exclamatory, (b) interrogative, (c) imperative, and (d) declarative. Recent linguistic research might question this analysis and substitute the three basic types with exclamation as an optional color.[19] At any rate, exclamatory sentences do not appear in normative systems and hence are of no interest in the analysis of normative discourse.

---

[16]At first glance it might appear that natural language can be represented as a conjunction of sentences. But as soon as one reflects that a single contradiction suffices to invalidate the conjunction, one realizes that such a view must be abandoned. The conception of natural language as a disjunction of conjunctions allows for the possibility of contradiction without the invalidation of the language system.

[17]For our analysis we shall take English as an arbitrary member of the class of natural languages and assume that analogous procedures can be established for the whole class.

[18]We shall take as our examples of sentences those carrying Judeo-Christian, Roman-law, and Anglo-American normative contents, assuming that analogous procedures can be established for other normative systems as well.

[19]I am indebted here to Professor Oldknow.

Interrogative sentences do not appear in normative codes, but they do appear in judicial proceedings and will therefore have to be considered in a comprehensive analysis of normative discourse. Let us then ask a hypothetical question in the law court: "Did you do it?" The respondent is forced to answer yes or no. This question amounts actually to the following compound sentence when properly expanded: *There is the respondent x and there is an act y such that x did do y or x did not do y; and it is not the case that x both did do y and did not do y*. The structure of this compound sentence is transparent. What the respondent is asked to do is to select the disjunct that fits the case. In a similar way every interrogative sentence used in judicial proceedings can be reduced to a compound declarative sentence, leaving open the selection blank for appropriate filling in. Interrogative sentences can thus be suitably paraphrased into declarative sentences and the whole problem of analysis of interrogative sentences reduced to that of declarative sentences.[20]

Imperative sentences do not appear often in normative discourse, quite contrary to what might be expected. But they do play an important role in it since they are used to express commands. There are no syntactic difficulties concerning imperative sentences, but the logical difficulties are considerable. Some of these are due to the introduction of metaphysical considerations which can be clearly separated and dealt with in their proper context. The introduction of these metaphysical considerations was due to the intimate connection between what metaphysicians of law and morals call judgments of value, norms, and imperatives. Some of these metaphysicians identify all of them, some identify norms and imperatives, and some distinguish all three as different normative categories.[21] And corresponding with these predilections, some develop systems of 'deontic logic' and some talk about 'logic of im-

---

[20]The problem of interrogative sentences is much more complex than it may appear. It was possible to simplify it here because the analysis of normative discourse does not necessitate going further into the problem. An interesting symposium on the broader issue involving interrogative sentences is offered by Sylvain Bromberger, "Questions," *The Journal of Philosophy*, LXIII, 220 (1966), pp. 597–606; David Harrah, "Question Generators," *ibid.*, pp. 606–608; and Nuel D. Belnap, Jr., "Questions, Answers, and Presuppositions," *ibid.*, pp. 609–611.

[21]Georges Kalinowski, *Introduction a la logique juridique* (Paris: R. Pichon and R. Durand-Auzias, 1965), pp. 59f.

peratives.' But none of them clearly distinguish linguistic expressions of normative discourse on the one hand from ontological entities, called norms, imperatives, and judgments of value, on the other hand. In order to avoid this confusion, and without prejudging metaphysical issues, the distinction will be made between imperative sentences as subjects of analysis and ontological entities called 'commands,' 'imperatives,' 'value judgments,' and 'norms,' which are not subject to the kind of analysis to be undertaken here.

Most normative discourse is made up of declarative sentences. A subclass of these, sometimes called 'normative' sentences, are used to express normative contents. Indeed, this subclass of declarative sentences and imperative sentences constitute the only kinds of sentences used to express normative contents.

'Normative' sentences are usually considered to be those that begin with the so-called deontic operators 'it is permitted that,' 'it is forbidden that,' and their equivalents. Whether such sentences as 'x has the right to do y,' 'x is good' are to be considered 'normative' sentences is a controversial issue. If the fact that a certain sentence expresses normative contents is considered as decisive, then not only all of these but also imperative sentences ought to be considered as 'normative' sentences. But, since we take syntactic structure as decisive in these initial considerations, imperative sentences will be excluded from the class of 'normative' sentences; but all declarative sentences expressing normative contents, irrespective of whether they have deontic operators or not, will be classified as 'normative' sentences.

Confusion of metaphysical with linguistic issues has taken place in the case of normative sentences just as in the case of imperative sentences. In this case also we shall separate linguistic expressions from ontological entities called norms and values. Therefore, there are no reasons from the syntactic viewpoint to treat normative sentences differently from other declarative sentences, although there are certain logical and semantic problems concerning normative sentences that will be discussed later.

5. Normative discourse, which is the expression of a normative system, consists of declarative and imperative sentences. The minimum requirement for any discourse to be counted as normative is that it contains at least one normative or at least one imperative sentence. Syntactic rules of natural language specify which of its linguistic expressions are to be counted as imperative and which as declarative sentences. A declarative sentence can be normative or non-normative. Every normative sentence must contain at least one normative word in order to count as a normative sentence.[22] If this specification is not met, a declarative sentence is to count as non-normative.

Normative discourse then is a proper subclass of natural language that contains:

(1) At least one imperative sentence and possibly an infinite number of them;

or

(2) At least one normative sentence and possibly an infinite number of them;

or

(3) At least one imperative and one normative sentence and possibly an infinite number of either of them;

or

(4) At least one imperative and one non-normative declarative sentence and possibly an infinite number of either of them;

or

(5) At least one normative and one non-normative declarative sentence and possibly an infinite number of either of them;

or

(6) At least one imperative, one normative, and one non-normative declarative sentence and possibly an infinite number of any of them.

IV. *Philosophical Analysis of Normative Discourse*

1. The pair of terms 'analysis' and 'analysandum,' collectively 'analysanda,' are correlative since every analysis must make the fundamental ontological assumption that the objects which it proposes to analyze exist in some form. The assumed existence of analysanda can be broadly or narrowly construed, on the basis of theoretical or practical criteria.

Analysanda differ from one realm to another and hence the

---

[22]Further specifications as to which words are to count as normative will be given later.

methods by which they can be analyzed will have to differ also. If it is assumed, as is indeed justified, that communication of analysanda must be formulable in some language, then two classes of analysanda will be distinguishable: ontological entities in the narrower sense, and linguistic expressions (which can also count as ontological entities, if "ontological entity" is understood in a broader sense). The analysis, therefore, can be performed on two levels: the level of language and the level of objects referred to by linguistic expressions. Hence the analysis of normative systems can also be performed on two levels, the level of language and the ontological level.[23] If the analysis is performed on the level of language, then its objective will be the analysis of the respective discourse, which is in our case normative discourse.

2. The goal of philosophical analysis of normative discourse is the clarification and explication of normative discourse on the one hand, and on the other hand the solution of the problem of meaning for the normatively significant components of normative discourse. Hence the philosophical analysis of normative discourse will devolve in two stages: the clarification of the logical structure of normative discourse by means of formal logic, and the clarification of the problem of meaning by formal or informal semantics.

3. Formal methods are, of course, preferable to informal methods, and the question of using informal methods at all may legitimately be raised. The overall reason is that formal methods do not suffice for a comprehensive analysis of normative discourse; for in order to effect a complete analysis, ontological entities must be correlated with the respective terms at appropriate junctures of formal analysis, and, since no formal methods for the analysis of ontological entities of normative discourse are known or are likely to be discovered, informal methods must be used for this purpose.

4. Contemporary philosophical investigations of normative discourse usually adhere to one or another method and approach, ignoring in most cases whatever contributions others may have to make. This is not the standard practice in investigations into law

---

[23]The analysis of normative systems on the language level is a necessary though not a sufficient condition for a complete interpretation of normative systems. Cf. on this point Ulrich Klug, *Juristische Logik* (2d rev. edn.; Berlin: Springer-Verlag, 1958), p. iv. This note is offered in response to Professor Allen, who wondered what good the analysis would be to the judge and the counsel.

and morals, and neither should it be in the investigation of normative discourse. We shall attempt to remedy this situation, though not by giving a systematic overall review of other approaches, but only the relevant methods and approaches that can be useful for the problems at hand. Formal logic and semantics methods will be assessed in the course of our investigation, as well as the approaches of ordinary language philosophy and phenomenology. If they are conducive to a successful analysis of the given problem of normative discourse, use will be made of them. If not, we shall attempt to devise our own methods in order to effect the solution of the problem.

Our position, therefore, can be characterized generally as a critical synthesis of other methods and approaches with our own. It must not, however, be confused with eclecticism, since our goal is not the construction of a system or theory for the analysis of normative discourse, which we do not believe to be possible, but rather a systematic attempt at the clarification and explication of the problems connected with discourse.

LOGICAL ANALYSIS OF NORMATIVE DISCOURSE

I. *The Logic of Non-normative Declarative Sentences*

1. The task of logical analysis of normative discourse consists in the explication of the logical structure of sentences appearing in it, and then in the analysis of logical relations between explicated sentences.

The explication of the logical structure of non-normative declarative sentences has been, within certain limitations, successfully accomplished. The analysis of logical relations between explicated non-normative declarative sentences has been brought to such perfection that the problem of logical relations between them has been reduced almost to a mechanical application of the techniques of symbolic logic.

There are still great difficulties in the explication of the logical structure of normative and imperative sentences, and therefore also in the analysis of logical relations between them. These difficulties will have to be overcome if the logical analysis of normative discourse is to be useful in normative pursuits, for it is an empirical fact that normative discourse contains normative, non-normative declarative, and imperative sentences. Hence a logical analysis that is to be useful must be able to establish which logical relations hold between the sentences appearing in it. This can be done only after the task of explication has been accomplished, and the logical relations that can hold between any two sentences of the normative discourse can be tabulated as follows:

(1) Logical relations between normative and normative sentences.

(2) Logical relations between normative and non-normative declarative sentences.

(3) Logical relations between normative and imperative sentences.

(4) Logical relations between imperative and imperative sentences.

13

(5) Logical relations between imperative and non-normative declarative sentences.

(6) Logical relations between non-normative and non-normative declarative sentences.

The task of explication of normative and imperative sentences, as well as the task of their logical relations, will be undertaken in the succeeding sections; the task of explication of non-normative declarative sentences, as well as their logical relations, will be undertaken in the ensuing portions of this section.

2. The logical explication of non-normative declarative sentences has been carried out magisterially as far as it will go by Willard Van Orman Quine.[1] There is in principle no more to be done, except to add this or that detail or make this or that adjustment to fit a particular purpose, and to point out the limitations of such explication.

The initial object of explication is the sentence; and the purpose of explication is to make possible the presentation of sentence in canonical notation. Regimentation is the process by which sentences are brought into a form suitable for presentation in canonical notation.[2] Paraphrase is the main method by which regimentation is accomplished,[3] and intuition is the main instrument of regimentation.[4] The sentence that has been prepared for canonical presentation is a regimented sentence. The process of regimentation amounts thus to the process of making sentences of natural language amenable to logical analysis.

The next objects of explication are components of sentences. The objective in this stage of explication is to regiment the sen-

---

[1] *Word and Object* (Cambridge: The M.I.T. Press, 1965).

[2] *Ibid.*, pp. 157 ff.

[3] *Ibid.* Cf. also Quine's *Methods of Logic* (New York: Holt, Rinehart and Winston, 1964), pp. 17ff., 40ff., 66f., 78, 85f., 92f., 124f., 131, 182ff., 205, 221ff.

[4] Quine does not use the word 'intuition,' but this is in effect what is presupposed by him. Moreover, provided one does not quibble about the interpretation of this vague word, Quine expresses the same idea elsewhere when he says: "A few clues to grouping in statements or ordinary language have been noted . . ., but in the main we must rely on our good sense of everyday idiom for a sympathetic understanding of the statement. . . ." Thus what Quine means by 'good sense of everyday idiom' and 'sympathetic understanding of the statement' are what we would mean by 'intuition' and 'intuitive grasp' of natural language. *Ibid.*, p. 44.

tential components into singular and general terms.[5] Once this is accomplished the regimentation of simple sentences is completed.

The last step that remains to be made in the process of regimentation is the paraphrasing of natural language connectives into the standard types amenable to truth-functional regimentation.

The basic types of simple and compound sentences that result after the regimentation has been completed are as follows:

(1) Simple non-normative declarative sentences, e.g., 'The snow is white.'

(2) Negated simple non-normative declarative sentences, e.g., 'It is not the case that the snow is white.'[6]

(3) Disjunction of simple non-normative declarative sentences, e.g., 'The snow is white or the snow is not white.'

(4) Conjunction of simple non-normative declarative sentences, e.g., 'The snow is white and the meadow is green.'

(5) Material conditional of simple non-normative declarative sentences, e.g., 'If the weather is nice, then Peter will go swimming.'[7]

---

[5]Singular terms could further be reduced to general terms. This reduction, however, is not desirable in so far as normative discourse is concerned. To appreciate the reasons, consider the sentence 'Justice is a virtue.' The singular term 'justice,' as well as others like it, would lose at least some of its normative significance by reduction to general terms.

[6]Complex problems that may arise in theoretical logic concerning negation are left out of consideration here since normative discourse is not affected by them. Cf. Haskell B. Curry, *Foundations of Mathematical Logic* (New York: McGraw-Hill, 1963), pp. 254–310, for a discussion of these problems.

[7]There are two controversial issues in connection with the material conditional: first, the issue of the so-called material implication (cf. Curry, pp. 250–253; Willard Van Orman Quine, *Mathematical Logic* [rev. ed.; New York: Harper and Row, 1962], pp. 14–18, 27–33; Quine, *Word and Object*, p. 226); and second, the issue of the counterfactual and subjunctive conditionals (cf. Quine, *Word and Object*, pp. 222–226; R. F. Tredwell, "The Problem of Counterfactuals," *Philosophy of Science*, Vol. XXXII, Nos. 3–4 [1965], 310-323).

The issue of material implication, if raised alone, is not in our opinion a legitimate one, since similar objections could be raised about any other connective, as well as the whole regimentation of natural language. If one bears in mind that regimentation of natural language does not involve a synonymous translation, but a paraphrase of natural language components in order to make them accessible to analysis, the issue disappears.

The issue of counterfactual and subjunctive conditionals, in so far as normative discourse is concerned, can be resolved by paraphrase, as elaborated by *Quine* (*Word and Object*, pp. 222-226). Counterfactual and subjunctive conditionals can thus be paraphrased into material conditional and possibly other sentences, depending on the context.

(6) Material biconditional of simple non-normative declarative
    sentences, e.g., 'Peter will go swimming if and only if the
weather is nice.'
(7) Universally quantified non-normative declarative sen-
    tences, e.g., 'All men are mortal.'
(8) Existentially quantified non-normative declarative sen-
    tences, e.g., 'Some women are blond.'[8]
(9) Quantifications of non-normative declarative sentences
    expressing relations, e.g., 'Everybody has a father.'

Any of the basic constructions, as well as the complex ones
constructed by means of them, can be abbreviated by using standard
logical symbols and presenting them in canonical notation. The
preceding examples abbreviated by means of canonical notation will
appear thus:[9]

(1) 'p'.
(2) '−p' ·
(3) 'p v −p'.
(4) 'p · q'.
(5) 'p ⊃ p'.
(6) 'p ≡ q'.
(7) '(x) (Fx ⊃ Gx)'.
(8) 'Ex) (Fx · Gx)'.
(9) '(Ex) (y) Fxy'.

Reduced thus to canonical notation, all non-normative declarative sentences show these basic constructions: predication, universal and existential quantification, and the truth functions. And
the ultimate components of such sentences are singular and general
terms which form in predication atomic open sentences.

----

[8]These basic types of sentences could further be reduced by well-known
logical techniques, but the reduced forms would be impractical for the purposes
of analyzing normative discourse.
    [9]The method of abbreviation rather than translation into symbols has been
extensively elaborated by Donald Kalish and Richard Montague, *Logic: Techniques
of Formal Reasoning* (New York: Harcourt, Brace and World, Inc., 1964), *passim*.
The method of abbreviating linguistic expressions is closer to our approach than
the standard method of translation, and hence will be adopted. In addition to
abbreviating sentences and terms of natural language as elaborated by Kalish and
Montague, we further introduce the symbols of truth-functional connectives, universal and existential quantification, as abbreviations of regimented 'and,' 'it is not
the case that,' 'if ... then,' 'or,' 'everything,' etc.

3. Quine's (and also any other) method of regimentation of natural language forces recalcitrant sentences and their components into a certain mold by shoving aside aspects of natural language that are not amenable to such treatment or are not relevant to analysis. This fact, together with the fact that regimentation rests ultimately on intuition, needs justification.

The fact that regimentation deals selectively with multifarious aspects of natural language, and, moreover, that it forces natural language into a certain preconceived mold, is not peculiar to logical explication and analysis of natural language, but to any analysis. Indeed, such a selectiveness is an advantage, so long as we remember that our analysis is selective and partial, for it is precisely the selectiveness that allows us to discern logical structures below the surface of natural language.

Reliance on intuition has often been subjected to criticism in twentieth-century philosophy. These criticisms were based mostly on an arbitrary understanding of the role of intuition in everyday life and even in science. There is no need to go further into this here except to point out that not only natural language, but also law and morals rest on the assumption that human beings can understand and "know" them intuitively. Any analysis of natural language as well as of law and morals has to accept this fact, and moreover will ultimately have to rest on intuition.

4. The last major problem regarding explication of non-normative declarative sentences is represented by sentences formed by means of the so-called modal operators 'it is necessary that...' and 'it is possible that . . .' Systems of modal logic have been developed in order to subject such sentences to logical explication and analysis. However, there are serious difficulties involved in connection with quantification into modal contexts which we need not go into here.[10] Two alternatives suggest themselves concerning

---

[10]Important works dealing with modal logic and these difficulties are: C. I. Lewis and C. H. Langford, *Symbolic Logic* (2d edn; New York: Dover Publications, 1959), pp. 492–502; R. C. Barcan, "A Functional Calculus Based on Strict Implication," *Journal of Symbolic Logic*, XI (1946), 1–16; Rudolf Carnap, *Meaning and Necessity* (Chicago: The University of Chicago Press, 1964), pp. 173–204; G. H. von Wright, *An Essay in Modal Logic* (Amsterdam: North Holland Publishing Co., 1951); Oskar Becker, *Untersuchungen über den Modalkalkül* (Meisenheim/Glan: Westkulturverlag Anton Hain, 1952); Jan Lukasiewicz, "A System of Modal Logic," *Journal of Computing Systems*, Vol. I, No. 3 (1953), 111–149; A.

the problem of modal sentences in so far as normative discourse is concerned: (1) to develop a modal logic adequate for normative discourse as a whole, i.e., a modal logic by means of which all sentences appearing in normative discourse would be analyzable, which in turn would mean abandonment of extensional language of the standard logic; or (2) to abandon modal logic altogether.[11]

Since modal logic without quantification would be almost useless for the logical analysis of normative discourse, the problem of quantifying into modal contexts would have to be resolved before modal logic could seriously be considered as a tool for normative-discourse analysis. Moreover, a comprehensive modal logic would have to be developed which was capable of handling not only modal sentences, but also imperative, normative, and other than modal non-normative sentences. And lastly, the complications that would ensue from abandoning extensional language cannot be minimized. All told, this alternative would present staggering problems to those who would wish to choose it.

The second alternative, known as the thesis of extensionality, has been advanced by Quine, and consists in the regimentation of intensional contexts and their reduction to extensional ones.[12] Since modal sentences seldom appear in normative discourse and since their explication in normative discourse along the lines suggested by Quine presents no difficulties, the second alternative suggests itself naturally to us.

5. Once the non-normative declarative sentences are regimented, the analysis of logical relations between them may be undertaken in order to establish the kind of logical relations which

N. Prior, *Formal Logic* (Oxford: The Clarendon Press, 1963), pp. 186–229; Paul Lorenzen, *Einführung in die Operative Logik und Mathematik* (Berlin: Springer Verlag, 1955), pp. 105–118; J. Hintikka, "The Modes of Modality," Acta Philosophica Fennica, XVI (1963), 65–82; Curry, *Foundations of Mathematical Logic*, pp. 359-368; R. Feys, *Modal Logics* (Louvain: E. Nauvelaerts, 1965).

[11] Williard Van Orman Quine's criticisms of modal logic are well-known and appear in "Reference and Modality," *From a Logical Point of View* (2d rev. edn.; Harper Torchbook, 1963), pp. 139–159; *Word and Object*, pp. 195–200, 202; and in Carnap's *Meaning and Necessity*, pp. 193–202. H. Scholz and G. Hasenjaeger, *Grundzüge der mathematischen Logik* (Berlin: Springer Verlag, 1961), pp. 14, 50, also hold no brief for modal logic.

[12] *Word and Object*, pp. 191–232. Rudolf Carnap also admits the possibility of this alternative (*Meaning and Necessity*, pp. 141-142, 172; *Introduction to Symbolic Logic and Its Applications* [New York: Dover Publications, 1958], p. 114).

hold between any finite number of them. A considerable number of first-order systems of logic, the only ones we need, are available for this purpose, and they can be arranged in the following four classes:[13]

(1) Classical systems having the syntactical approach.
(2) Classical systems using the semantic approach.
(3) Jaskowski-Gentzen systems using the syntactic approach.
(4) Jaskowski-Gentzen systems using the semantic approach.

The choice from among any of these will depend on practical rather than theoretical considerations. The systems using the semantic approach are closer to the reasoning of everyday life and the normative sphere. And, since in these there is no need to entertain scruples regarding semantic notions, semantically built systems are to be preferred. Jaskowski-Gentzen types of systems using natural deduction are again to be preferred because of their nearness to the way of reasoning in everyday life and the normative sphere. Therefore, the most suitable systems for the purposes of logical analysis of normative discourse are the ones that are built semantically and use natural deduction.[14]

Once the system of logic has been selected, the ultimate task of the logical analysis of normative discourse—provided that normative and imperative sentences can suitably be treated—can be performed; which is to find out whether any of the following relations hold between any finite number of sentences of normative discourse:

(1) The relation of implication.
(2) The relation of equivalence.
(3) The relation of compatibility or incompatibility.

II. *The Logic of Normative Sentences*

1. Normative sentences fall into five classes:

(a) Declarative sentences, one or more of whose components are normative words, and which have the forms 'Fa,' '—Fa,' '(x) (Fx $\supset$ Gx),' '(x) (Fx $\supset$ —Gx),' '(Ex) (Fx $\cdot$ Gx),' and '(Ex) (Fx $\cdot$ — Gx)'; 'Peter is an honorable man,' 'Justice is a virtue.'

---

[13]Intuitionist systems are omitted, since the issue of intuitionist vs. classical logic has no bearing on normative discourse.

[14]Quine's *Methods of Logic* suggests itself as the most suitable of these.

(b) Normative sentences formed by means of what will be called here deontic predicates, which are of the forms 'Fa,' '–Fa,' '(x) (Fx ⊃ Gx),' '(x) (Fx ⊃ —Gx),' '(Ex) (Fx · Gx),' '(Ex) (Fx · —Gx),' and '(x₁) ...(xₙ) (Fx₁, ..., xₙ)'; e.g., 'A ought to do b,' 'Gambling is unlawful.'

(c) Normative sentences constructed by means of the so-called deontic operators of the form 'It is . . . that . . .'; e.g., 'It is permitted that the passengers disembark.'

(d) Normative sentences constructed by means of deontic operators of the form 'It is . . . to . . .'; e.g., 'It is forbidden to loiter on the premises.'

(e) Normative sentences constructed by means of deontic operators of the form 'It is . . . for . . .'; e.g., 'It is unlawful for pedestrians to cross the street.'

The first class of normative sentences is subject to the same kind of explication and analysis as non-normative declarative sentences. Hence a further discussion of them is unnecessary and can be omitted. The last four classes of sentences can be involved in the problems of deontic logic and will, therefore, need special attention. For this reason a discussion of deontic logic will be introduced and its possible relation to our scheme of things determined; afterwards a fresh attempt at the solution of the problem of explication and analysis of these sentences will be undertaken.

2. Deontic logic can be said to have been inaugurated by G. H. von Wright's article "Deontic Logic,"[15] although a few attempts can be registered before this one.[16] Subsequent investigations into deontic logic by von Wright himself,[17] O. Becker,[18] A. R. Anderson, [19] Georges (Jerzy) Kalinowski, [20] Hector-Neri Castañeda,[21] Jaakko Hintikka,[22] A. N. Prior,[23] Nicholas Rescher,[42] Mark Fischer,[25] Roderick Chisholm,[26] E. J. Lemmon,[27] and F. B. Fitch[28]

---

[15]*Mind*, LX (1951), 1–15.

[16]Kalinowski, *Introduction*, pp. 73ff.

[17]*An Essay in Modal Logic* (Amsterdam: North Holland Publishing Co., 1951), pp. 1–4, 36–41; "A Note on Deontic Logic and Derived Obligation," *Mind* LXV (1956), 507–509; *Norm and Action* (London: Routledge and Kegan Paul, 1957).

[18]*Untersuchungen über den Modalkalkül* (Meisenheim/Glan: West-Kultur-verlag Anton Hain, 1952), pp. 37–50. Becker was not familiar with von Wright's article, but his "normative interpretation of the modal calculus" belongs to the writings on deontic logic, and is indeed nothing but a variant of deontic logic.

(who was the first to employ natural deduction rules in deontic logic), move more or less along the lines laid out by von Wright's articles on deontic logic.

Deontic logic is at best in an inchoate stage, so much so that even its purpose and aims cannot be determined which clarity.[29] Thus some deontic logicians consider deontic logic to be simply a branch of modal logic, some consider it to be independent of modal logic, and some consider it to be an extension of modal logic. Moreover, there is not even agreement among the architects of deontic logic as to what is its province. Some of them think it to be value judgments, imperatives, and norms, some single out imperatives and norms, and some only norms. Since most deontic logicians consider norms to be the special province of deontic logic, and since it is norms that are of interest in our scheme of things at the moment, we shall restrict deontic logic to this province.

---

[19]"The Formal Analysis of Normative Systems," Technical Report No. 2 (unpublished manuscript), Interaction Laboratory, Sociology Department of Yale University, 1956; Alan Ross Anderson and Omar Khayyam Moore, "The Formal Analysis of Normative Concepts," *American Sociological Review*, XXII (1957), 9–17; "A Reduction of Deontic Logic to Alethic Modal Logic," *Mind*, LXVII (1958), 100–103.

[20]"Théorie des Propositions Normatives," *Studia Logica*, I (1953), 146–182; and *Introduction*.

[21]"A Theory of Morality," *Philosophy and Phenomenological Research*, XVII (1956), 339–352; "On the Logic of Norms," *Methodos*, IX (1957), 207–216; "The Logic of Obligation," *Philosophical Studies*, X (1959), 17–23; "Obligation and Modal Logic," *Logique et Analyse*, III (1960), 40–48; "Outline of a Theory on the General Logical Structure of the Language of Action," *Theoria*, XXI (1960), 151–182.

[22]"Quantifiers in Deontic Logic," *Societas Scientiarum Fennica, Commentationes Humanarum Literarum*, XXIII, No. 4 (1957), 1–23.

[23]*Formal Logic*, pp. 220–229; "A Note on the Logic of Obligation," *Revue Philosophique de Louvain*, 1960, pp. 86–87; *Time and Modality* (Oxford: The Clarendon Press, 1957); "Logic, Deontic," *The Encyclopedia of Philosophy*, IV (1967), 509–513.

[24]"An Axiom System for Deontic Logic," *Philosophical Studies*, IX (1958), 24–30; "Conditional Permission in Deontic Logic," *Philosophical Studies*, XIII (1962), 1–6.

[25]"A System of Deontic-Alethic Modal Logic," *Mind*, LXXI (1962), 231–236.

[26]"The Ethics of Requirement," *American Philosophical Quarterly*, I (1964), 147-153.

[27]"Deontic Logic and the Logic of Imperatives," *Logique et Analyse*, VIII (1965), 39–71.

[28]"Natural Deduction Rules for Obligation," *American Philosophical Quarterly*, III (1966), 27–37.

[29]Cf. Kalinowski's *Introduction*, pp. 137ff. for an assessment of the present state of deontic logic.

But the crucial question that must be raised and answered is: What is the purpose of deontic logic? On this depends whether or not the whole idea of deontic logic ought to be pursued, and if so, in what direction and to what extent. In order to obtain an answer to this question we shall cull the writings of deontic logicians for statements about the purpose of the subject they are pursuing, and on the basis of these try to draw a conclusion as to the purpose of deontic logic.

(a) The purpose of deontic logic according to von Wright is the study of ". . . propositions (and truth-functions of propositions(about the obligatory, permitted, forbidden, and other (derivative) deontic characters of acts (and performance-functions of acts)."[30]

(b) A. R. Anderson expresses the purpose of deontic logic in this way:

> It should be emphasized that the chief value of formalizing a logic of norms, or indeed any logic at all, does *not* lie simply in the use of shorthand notational devices, though an economical symbolism can be helpful. The idea is not to "translate" from one language into another, but rather to express propositions in a language the logical structure of which is explicit and definite. An adequate formalization makes it possible to check in a detailed and rigorous way just what follows from what, and such rigorous checking is an obvious prerequisite for the use of the axiomatic approach.[31]

(c) This is A. N. Prior's way of expressing it: "Deontic logic, or the logic of obligation, is that area of thought in which we formulate and systematize such principles as that nothing can be obligatory and forbidden at once and that whatever we are committed to by doing what is obligatory is itself obligatory."[32]

(d) G. Kalinowski puts it as follows: "Car la logique déontique étudie les relations constantes formelles existant entre les propositions normatives, quelle que soient les normes signifiées par ces propositions.[33]

---

[30]"Deontic Logic," p. 5.
[31]"The Formal Analysis of Normative Concepts," p. 12 footnote.
[32]"Logic, Deontic," p. 509.
[33]*Introduction*, p. 70.

No detailed criticism of the proposed purpose of deontic logic or of deontic logic itself need be registered here.[34] But these fundamental questions must be raised:

(1) Is it necessary to create deontic logic in order to investigate "propositions about the obligatory," or to formalize logical relations among such propositions? Could not the standard logic suffice for such a purpose?

(2) Even if such a formalization of deontic propositions could adequately be accomplished, which remains to be shown, how would deontic propositions formalized in such a way fit with propositions formalized by standard logic? For if a complete formalization of normative discourse is to be effected, then a super system of logic would have to be created in order to accommodate not only deontic but all other sentences.

These are the questions that will have to be answered and the issues raised by them settled before deontic logic can be seriously considered as an instrument for logical analysis of normative discourse. At present, therefore, deontic logic can at best be used for a partial logical analysis of a minute portion of normative discourse. Hence two avenues remain open if a complete logical analysis of normative discourse is to be effected: (a) the development of a super logic that would be able to deal effectively with all of the problems of normative-discourse logical analysis; or (b) the exploration of possibilities for handling the problems of logical analysis of normative sentences by means of standard logic.

Since the first avenue is beset with enormous difficulties and complications, it will not recommend itself if it can be shown that standard logic suffices for the purposes of logical analysis of normative sentences. Hence it will suffice for the solution of the problem of logical analysis of normative sentences if it can be shown that standard logic can indeed deal effectively with the problem of logical analysis of normative sentences. To show that standard logic can deal effectively with normative sentences, we must show that the extensionalist thesis holds for them, which amounts to showing that normative sentences can be formalized by means of an extensional language.

----

[34]Such a one has been offered by Lemmon. *Logique et Analyse*, VIII, 43–52.

3. Normative sentences formed by means of deontic predicates fall into two subclasses:

(a) Normative sentences formed by means of one-place deontic predicates, e.g., 'Gambling is unlawful.'

(b) Normative sentences formed by means of n–place (n > or equal to 2) deontic predicates, e.g., 'Ex) (Ey) (x ought to do y).'

The extensions of terms in the sentences of subclass (a) are clearly classes of which the respective terms are true or false. The extensions of terms of the sentences of subclass (b) are ordered n-tuples of which the respective terms are again clearly true or false. No opaque constructions are involved in connection with both subclasses of these sentences, and hence they are formalizable by means of an extensional language in a straightforward way. Therefore the extensionalist thesis holds for them.

4. Normative sentences constructed by means of deontic operators of the form 'It is . . . that . . .' are the result of applying such operators on sentences. Since all deontic operators of this form can be defined by means of the deontic operator 'It is permitted that . . . ,' it will suffice to deal with this operator only. Moreover, since the complete analysis of an arbitrary example of such sentences applies to all of them, it will suffice to perform it on just one of them. We choose as an example of such a sentence 'It is permitted that the passengers disembark.' There are altogether four possible constructions of such a sentence by means of the components and their negations:

(1) It is permitted that the passengers disembark.
(2) It is permitted that the passengers do not disembark.
(3) It is not permitted that the passengers disembark.
(4) It is not permitted that the passengers do not disembark.

These sentences cannot be formalized by means of an extensional language as they stand.[35] Furthermore the constructions of these compounds are opaque in that the truth values of the compounds are not affected in the same way as they would be in an extensional language by the change in the truth values of the sen-

---

[35]The usual formalization of them in propositional deontic logic is as follows (letting 'P' stand for 'It is permitted that...' and 'p' for 'The passengers disembark'): (1) Pp; (2) P–p; (3) –Pp; (4) –P–p.

tence 'The passengers disembark.' Thus 'It is permitted that the passengers disembark' and 'It is permitted that the passengers do not disembark' are not contradictory. On the other hand, 'It is not permitted that the passengers disembark' and 'It is not permitted that the passengers do not disembark' are contradictory. The truth value of the compound is not affected by the change of the truth values of 'The passengers disembark' in the first case, but it is affected in the second case. Hence the substitutivity of identity would fail in that the substitution of the true sentence 'The passengers disembark' by its negation and vice versa need not affect the truth value of the compound. The extensionalist thesis, therefore, does not hold for this sentence as it stands and the standard logic cannot be applied for its analysis.

However, if these four sentences are paraphrased in the following way, and if we assume that the paraphrasing is correct, such paraphrases result in sentences formed by means of deontic predicates for which the extensionalist thesis holds.

(1) Disembarking of passengers is permitted.
(2) Not disembarking of passengers is permitted.
(3) Disembarking of passengers is not permitted.
(4) Not disembarking of passengers is not permitted.

We may conclude, therefore, that the logical analysis of normative sentences constructed by means of the deontic operators 'It is . . . that . . .' is possible by standard logic, provided that the method of paraphrase is accepted and that the paraphrasing in the given instance is correct.

5. Normative sentences constructed by means of the deontic operators 'It is . . . to . . .' are the result of applying these operators on terms. Since these operators are interdefinable, the analysis performed on one of them will suffice for all of them. We choose the operator 'It is forbidden to . . .' and the sentence 'It is forbidden to loiter on the premises' for the purposes of analysis.

If the example 'It is forbidden to loiter on the premises' is developed, the following four possibilities arise:

(1) It is forbidden to loiter on the premises.
(2) It is forbidden not to loiter on the premises.

(3) It is not forbidden to loiter on the premises.

(4) It is not forbidden not to loiter on the premises.[36]

Normative sentences formed by means of the operator 'It is forbidden to . . .' can be paraphrased as follows:

(1) Loitering on the premises is forbidden.

(2) Not loitering on the premises is forbidden.

(3) Loitering on the premises is not forbidden.

(4) Not loitering on the premises is not forbidden.

The logical structure of sentences formed by means of the operator 'It is forbidden to . . .' is laid bare when thus paraphrased, and they appear simply as disguised forms of normative sentences constructed by means of the deontic predicates. The extensionalist thesis therefore holds for these sentences, and they can be formalized in a straightforward way as follows:

(1)   (x) (Fx ⊃ Gx).

(2)   (x) (—Fx ⊃ Gx).

(3)   (x) (Fx ⊃ —Gx).

(4)   (x) (—Fx ⊃ —Gx).

6. Normative sentences constructed by means of the deontic operators 'It is . . . for . . .' are the result of applying these operators to terms. Since all of these deontic operators are interdefinable it will suffice to resolve the problem of analysis for one of them. We choose the operator 'It is unlawful for . . .' and the sentence 'It is unlawful for pedestrians to cross the street' as examples for analysis. These are the possible constructions of the sentence:

(1) It is unlawful for pedestrians to cross the street.

(2) It is unlawful for pedestrians not to cross the street.

(3) It is not unlawful for pedestrians to cross the street.

(4) It is not unlawful for pedestrians not to cross the street.

Paraphrasing of these sentences will lay bare their logical structure:

(1) Crossing of the street by pedestrians is unlawful.

(2) Not crossing of the street by pedestrians is unlawful.

(3) Crossing of the street by pedestrians is not unlawful.

(4) Not crossing of the street by pedestrians is not unlawful.

---

[36]Deontic logicians usually formalize these sentences in the following way (taking 'p' to stand for the act of loitering on the premises and 'F' for the deontic operator 'It is forbidden . . .'): Fp; (2) F—p; (3) —Fp; (4) —F—p.

The extensionalist thesis holds also for this class of normative sentences, and their formalization can be effected in the same way as the formalization of sentences constructed by means of the operator "It is forbidden to . . .'.

7. The extensionalist thesis holds, therefore, for all normative sentences, assuming that their paraphrasing is legitimate and correct. Hence standard first-order logic suffices for all of the purposes of their logical analysis. If we assume, as we are indeed justified in assuming on empirical grounds, that normative contents must be expressible by means of natural language in order to play a role in the normative realm, then standard first-order logic suffices for all of the purposes of law and morals. Deontic logic can therefore be dispensed with in the logical investigation of normative discourse, normative systems, and normative theories. On the other hand, deontic logic can still be useful for the analysis of certain normative sentences and normative relations in general when we wish to proceed directly with their formalization without first having to resort to the techniques of paraphrase.

III. *The Logic of Imperative Sentences*

1. Investigations into the logical structure of imperative sentences have been obfuscated by metaphysical issues, as well as by the failure to take into consideration significant elucidations of the grammatical structure of imperative sentences made by linguists. Starting off with these disadvantages, the logic of imperatives or the logic of commands has been initiated within the past three decades.

The first significant attempt to formalize the logic of imperatives was made by Albert Hofstadter and J. C. C. McKinsey.[37] Several more recent attempts along the same or somewhat different lines include works by Hector-Neri Castañeda,[38] E. J. Lemmon,[39] J. B. Keene,[40] and Nicholas Rescher.[41] Basic to the approach of all

---

[37]"On the Logic of Imperatives," *Philosophy of Science*, VI (1939), 446–457.

[38]"A Theory of Morality," *Philosophy and Phenomenological Research*, XVII (1956), 339–352.

[39]"Deontic Logic and the Logic of Imperatives," *Logique et Analyse*, VIII (1965), 39–71.

[40]"Can Commands Have Logical Consequences?", *American Philosophical Quarterly*, III, No. 1 (1966), 57-63.

[41]*The Logic of Commands* (London: Routledge and Kegan Paul, 1966).

of them is the assumption of existence of "imperatives," "norms," and "actions," which some clearly distinguish and some do not. None of them clearly distinguish between "imperatives" and the linguistic expressions called imperative sentences, by means of which the former are supposedly expressed. Nor do any of these treatments pay serious attention to the grammatical complexities involved in the imperative sentences of natural language, and only Lemmon and Rescher pay attention to the semantic complexities involved in imperative sentences.

No detailed criticism of the logic of imperatives need be offered here, since even its recent architects, notably Lemmon and Rescher,[42] admit that it is still in an inchoate stage and that much has to be done before it can become a useful tool of normative analysis, granted that the approach itself is correct. But it is precisely the approach to imperative logic by preceding investigators that we shall challenge, and therewith also the logic of imperatives that they have been trying to develop. To be more specific, the position taken by us differs from that taken in preceding investigations in these respects:

(a) We refuse to make any initial ontological commitments in regard to 'imperatives'; we shall not postulate either that they exist or do not exist.

(b) Our attention will be directed to imperative sentences as linguistic expressions, and the goal of our enterprise will be the logical analysis of them as they appear in natural language.[43] And, as they stand, imperative sentences are one-word or n-word elliptic sentences that contain implicit logical structures which must be laid bare before proceeding with the logical analysis of them.[44]

---

[42]For detailed criticisms of previous works in the logic of imperatives, cf. Lemmon, *Logique et Analyse*, VIII, 55ff.; and for the general assessment of the present situation in the logic of imperatives, cf. Rescher, pp. 123f.

[43]The position of R. M. Hare, *The Language of Morals* (Oxford: The Clarendon Press, 1961), and Shia Moser, "Some Remarks about Imperatives," *Philosophy and Phenomenological Research*, XVII (1956), 186–206, is in this respect similar to ours, except that our ultimate goal is the formal analysis of imperative sentences, whereas Hare and Moser confine themselves to an informal analysis of imperative sentences.

[44]It is not amiss to indicate that the philosophical grammarians of Port Royal and contemporary linguists have discerned some aspects of this problem, although our analysis is independent and different from theirs. Cf. Noam Chomsky, *Cartesian Linguistics* (New York: Harper and Row, 1966), pp. 46ff. Cf. also Jerrold J. Katz, *The Philosophy of Language* (New York: Harper and Row, 1966), pp. 135ff.

2. One-word elliptic imperative sentences are the shortest imperative sentences. A standard grammatical, lexical, and contextual analysis discloses an infinite number of possible interpretations for such sentences. Such an analysis on a paradigmatic one-word imperative sentence, 'Go!', is as follows:

(a) Introducing the verbal form '... order ... to go' and using only pronouns to fill the blanks, over fifty possible interpretations are opened up; e.g., 'I order you to go,' 'You order him to go,' 'They order him to go.'

(b) Introducing variants formed by means of 'command' instead of 'order' doubles the number of possible interpretations using only pronouns to fill the blanks.

(c) Introducing further paraphrases of sentences obtained by the preceding methods increases substantially the number of alternative interpretations.

(d) Introducing names and descriptions to fill the blanks in addition to the pronouns allows an infinite number of possible interpretations.

Which ones of the possible interpretations are permissible will depend entirely upon the context. Moreover, it will also depend on the context which of the possible interpretations are true or false. The sentence 'Go!' itself is neither true nor false, as indeed no imperative sentence is capable of being true or false.

The imperative sentence 'Go!', when explicated and interpreted by means of the open sentence 'x orders y to go,' behaves like the open sentences 'x paid y to go' or 'x paid y to mow the lawn.' In other words, when the variables of the interpreted imperative sentence 'Go!' are replaced by constants or quantified, the replacement or quantification depending on contextual specifications, this interpreted imperative sentence becomes true or false, as the case may be, and thus subject to the standard logical analysis.

Since the one-word elliptic imperative sentence 'Go!' is a paradigm, we may now generalize and conclude that an explication and interpretation can be performed on any one-word elliptic imperative sentence; and hence that all one-word elliptic imperative sentences are subject to standard logical analysis subsequent to their contextual explication and interpretation.[45]

---

[45]It is important in this connection to stress that we are not "reducing im-

3. N-word (n > 2) elliptic imperative sentences will be introduced by means of the following paradigmatic examples:

(a) Obey the law!

(b) Don't talk so loud!

(c) If it is raining, close the door.[46]

(d) Heads of departments will submit their estimates before January first.[47]

(e) Let us pray.

(f) You shall not kill![48]

(g) This constitution shall take effect and be in full force immediately upon the admission of the territory as a state.[49]

(h) You must do it!

We proceed now with the explication and interpretation of n-word elliptic imperative sentences by interpreting the adduced paradigms.

(a) The imperative sentence 'Obey the law' is a two-word elliptic imperative sentence. (The definite article 'the' does not count as a word. Both definite and indefinite articles are idiosyncrasies of the English language and do not affect substantially the interpretation of the logical structure of this imperative sentence.) The number of possible interpretations of this sentence is infinite: thus, for example, 'I order you to obey the law,' 'Peter orders Paul to obey the law,' etc. The introduction of verbal forms, variants, paraphrases, names, and descriptions is performed in the same way as for one-word elliptic imperative sentences. Also, which possible interpretations are correct will depend entirely upon the context.

(b) The modern English 'Do-forms' of imperative sentences are easily reduced to older English imperative sentences without

---

peratives to indicatives," but interpreting imperative sentences. Attempts to reduce imperatives to indicatives have been sharply criticized by Hare (pp. 5ff.), and justly so if one has in mind the reduction of imperative sentences to declarative sentences. They cannot be reduced in such a fashion, and even declarative sentences cannot be reduced to other declarative sentences if one has in mind all of the natural language components. Natural language is too rich to allow that sort of manipulation.

[46]This example is borrowed from Lemmon, *Logique et Analyse*, VIII, 63.

[47]This example is borrowed from George O. Curme, *English Grammar* (New York: Barnes and Noble, 1957), p. 250, par. 116 D.

[48]Ex. 20 : 13, Revised Standard Version.

[49]North Dakota, *Constitution*, Schedule, Sec. 11.

the 'Do.' Thus the sentence 'Don't talk so loud' reduces to the older 'Talk not so loud,' and hence to the same paradigm as 'Obey the law.'

(c) The consequent of the conditional 'If it is raining, close the door,' is an instance of the paradigm 'Obey the law' and can be treated in the same way. Hence the whole conditional can be paraphrased into a declarative sentence and treated as such.

(d) The sentence 'Heads of departments will submit their estimates before January first' again allows an infinite number of interpretations on the basis of the following verbal forms:

(1) Heads of departments are ordered by . . . to submit their estimates before January first.

(2) . . . orders (or order) heads of departments to submit their estimates before January first.

The context in this case again will determine which of the possible interpretations are permissible. But here too the interpretation of the imperative sentence is given in terms of a declarative sentence or sentences, and hence this paradigmatic imperative sentence is subject to the standard logical analysis.

(e, f, g, h) These cases can be handled analogously to the preceding ones.

4. We have established now that interpretations of imperative sentences can be rendered by means of declarative sentences, and hence can be handled by means of standard logic. Our demonsstrations were shown to hold for paradigmatic cases of imperative sentences. On the basis of demonstrations holding for paradigmatic cases of imperative sentences, we generalize and conclude that all imperative sentences can be subjected to the same kind of interpretations.

There is no known and acceptable method of performing a direct logical analysis on imperative sentences. Moreover, one cannot be found, since imperative sentences amount essentially to open sentences which can be closed only contextually and not by means of logical rules; and without the closure of open sentences, no logical analysis in terms of implication, validity, and consistency can be performed. It is primarily for this reason, i.e., the failure to realize that imperative sentences have elliptical structure which can be completed only by contextual analysis, that preceding attempts to develop the logic of imperatives have failed.

IV. *The Metalogic of Normative Discourse*

1. It may be said without exaggeration that the development of modern formal logic was conditioned almost exclusively by problems in the foundations of mathematics. And since the problems of mathematics have dominated the development of formal logic to such an extent, it is not surprising that the major contributions to formal logic come from mathematicians. Incidental though the interest was in other than mathematical problems in the development of modern formal logic, its methods, techniques, and results do have a bearing on other than mathematical problems, and in particular on the problems of normative systems.

Although the methods, techniques, and results of modern logic do have a bearing on the problems of normative discourse, there are some central logical and metalogical issues that are only of an indirect interest to the normative realm,[50] and there are some others that are of concern primarily in the normative realm. It is the task of the metalogic of normative discourse to sift such issues and to explore those that are of concern in the normative realm.

2. Normative systems are developed intuitively just as systems of mathematics are. But unlike mathematical systems, normative systems do not lend themselves to formalization. Again the ideal way of presenting any system is the formal theory, provided that logical considerations play the decisive role in such formulations, as is the case in mathematics. The reasons for this situation are clear and obvious: the architects of mathematical systems assume logical considerations to be the determining factor in the formulations of their systems. The conscious or unconscious architects of normative systems, however, do not allow logical considerations to be the determining factor in their formulations. Even contradictions within normative systems can be tolerated.[51] Hence the construction of the formal theory of a normative system is precluded by the very assumptions of their architects.

The question now arises: If normative systems cannot be organized as formal theories, is it not possible to organize them in-

---

[50]Such issues are those involved in the controversy between Logicism, Intuitionism, and Formalism. Cf. Stephen Cole Kleene, *Introduction to Metamathematics* (New York: D. Van Nostrand Co., 1952), pp. 36–65, for a discussion of these and related issues.

[51]For such an example cf. Jovan Brkić, *Moral Concepts in Traditional Serbian Epic Poetry* ('S-Gravenhage: Mouton & Co., 1961), pp. 61ff.

formally? The answer to this question is affirmative, and indeed empirically known normative systems are organized informally and intuitively in more or less coherent systems; and informal and intuitive logic is customarily used in reasoning about such systems.

But, though normative systems are not presented in the form of formal theories, formal methods can (as we have endeavored to show) and should be used as an instrument for normative analysis. Application of formal methods is one of the most effective means of terminating debates involving logical factors, and there is no need to deprive law and morals of such instruments.

3. Metalogic, as it is customarily understood, takes formal systems as objects of its study.[52] Since normative systems cannot be formalized, it is clear that metalogic cannot play in this sense a significant role in the normative realm. On the other hand there are a few metalogical problems that are not only of great interest in the normative realm, but acquire peculiar twists and even solutions in it.

4. We now introduce fundamental concepts of the metalogic of normative discourse:

(a) Since normative discourse (and we remember that normative systems are expressed by means of normative discourse) is a disjunction of conjunctions, let it be counted as minimally consistent if and only if at least one of its disjuncts is consistent; and let it be counted as maximally consistent if and only if all of its disjuncts are consistent.

(b) Let the normative discourse be counted as minimally acceptable if and only if it is not minimally consistent. For it must then be possible to decide which contradictory components of such a disjunct are to be retained and which rejected. And let the normative discourse be counted as maximally acceptable if and only if every of its disjuncts is inconsistent. For again it must then be possible to decide for each of its disjuncts which of its components are to be rejected and which are to be retained.

5. It is possible by formal methods alone to decide effectively if the normative discourse is minimally consistent by inspection of any of its disjuncts with n (n > 1) components. But it would be impossible to decide this issue by inspection in the case of hypothetical disjunct which has an infinite number of components. It

---

[52]Kleene, p. 61f.

is also possible to decide if the normative discourse is maximally consistent in the case of a finite disjunction, but it is impossible to decide this by inspection in the case of an infinite disjunction.

Since it is an empirical fact that only finite disjunctions and conjunctions are involved in concrete normative discourse, it can in principle be decided whether or not any concrete normative discourse is minimally or maximally consistent.

6. Since it is possible to decide whether any concrete normative discourse is minimally or maximally consistent, it is also possible to decide whether it is minimally or maximally acceptable.

However, the decision as to which components of a minimally or maximally acceptable normative discourse are to be rejected and which retained cannot be made by inspection. In the case of law it is the law courts or legislatures that decide which of the two contradictory sentences of the given legal system is to be retained and which rejected. In the case of morals it is left to individual and social decision. The decision problem has a solution in this sense in the normative realm, though not by formal means.

In concrete terms the preceding remarks amount to the following: It is possible in normative discourse to determine for any arbitrary sentences of finite length if they are consistent or not by formal means only. Moreover, it is possible to decide which of the contradictory sentences are to be retained and which rejected in a normative discourse and hence in a normative system. This decision, however, can be reached only by extralogical means.

7. We now introduce the following additional metalogical concepts of normative discourse:

(a) A normative discourse shall be called ideal if it is maximally consistent.

(b) A normative discourse shall be called intolerable if it is minimally acceptable.

(c) And let the cleaning process be considered the transformation of acceptable disjuncts into consistent ones.

Then the fundametnal task of the logical analysis of normative discourse consists in the discovery of acceptable disjuncts, and the fundamental normative task consists in the transformation of acceptable disjuncts into consistent ones until the maximally consistent normative discourse is realized.

SEMANTIC ANALYSIS OF NORMATIVE DISCOURSE

I. *The Scope of Semantic Analysis of Normative Discourse*

The logical analysis of normative discourse represents only half of the philosophical analysis of normative discourse. In addition to the logical problems of normative discourse, there are problems of meaning and reference of singular and general terms, as well as certain psychological, sociocultural, and ontological problems which have to be aired before a complete philosophical analysis is effected. These we consider to be within the scope of the semantic analysis of normative discourse.

The goal of the semantic analysis of normative discourse can be said to be the solution of the problem of meaning for normative discourse. But the complete solution of meaning for normative discourse would, if it is to be presented in terms of a formal semantic theory, entail the complete solution of epistemological and metaphysical problems. This has not yet been realized and is hardly to be expected. Enormous efforts have been made in this direction in twentieth-century philosophy, but without success or even a reasonable chance of success. The reasons for this failure, in our opinion, include the arbitrarily high goals set for such a solution, and the unreasonably stringent stress placed on formal methods in much of twentieth-century philosophy.

But, although no formal semantic theory can be presented that has realized a complete solution of the problem of meaning, an intuitive and informal approach can be introduced that will be systematic enough to deal coherently with the range of problems of interest to normative discourse and elastic enough to be able to incorporate the positive contributions of other attempts made in this respect. We shall call this intuitive and informal approach phenomenological, since the phenomenological approach in philosophy is closest to our own, but we shall exclude the dogmatic and arbitrary screening out of other approaches merely because they do not happen to agree with the general phenomenological position. In the following pages, therefore, the phenomenological approach to the problem of meaning will be presented as a general framework with-in which individual contributions by other approaches will be incorporated if they stand scrutiny, and ontological issues in connection with the problem of meaning for normative discourse will be aired.

II. *The Phenomenological Approach to Normative Discourse*

1. The phenomenological approach to meaning is essentially an intuitive approach, although more elaborate and carried on by use of the phenomenological method.[1] The intuitive approach assumes that the meaning of natural language constants is 'known' by 'intuition,' or 'feeling,' or both. Implicit in this approach is the assumption that the speaker and the listener of a natural language 'know' the language, in which knowledge is included the common experience and knowledge of norms and values of the given language community.[2] This is a simple and naive approach in so far as the general theory of meaning is concerned.

Naive though it may be, however, it cannot be dismissed, for this reason: Assuming that law and morals are primary instruments of social control, as indeed they can easily be shown to be empirically, it must also be assumed that the members of a given society must understand the language of the law and morals by which they are to be controlled. It is true, of course, that there are intricate laws which are accessible only to initiates, but even these presuppose some basic laws which are assumed to be accessible to the 'normal' members of the language community. Therefore, any theory of meaning, if it is to have relevance for law and morals, cannot take as its task the dismissal of the intuitive approach, but must explain the intuitive understanding of normative words and make them as precise as possible.

This justification of the use of intuition in normative discourse contains, however, a criticizable kernel that will be shared by any

---

[1]The most significant works by the phenomenologists in so far as the theory of meaning is concerned are: Maurice Merleau-Ponty, *Signes* (Paris: Gallimard, 1960); Mikel Dufrenne, *Language and Philosophy*, trans. H. B. Veatch (Bloomington: Indiana University Press, 1963); and J. N. Mohanty, *Edmund Husserl's Theory of Meaning* (The Hague: Martinus Nijhoff, 1964).

[2]Empirical linguistics also recognizes this fact, for the discussion of which we refer to Katz, *Philosophy of Language, passim.*

approach to the problem of meaning that relies solely on intuition. Intuitive understanding of normative words is sometimes more, sometimes less vague, but it is seldom 'wrong'; and in most cases in everyday life as well as in scholarship we have neither time, desire, nor need to search for a more precise or 'right' understanding of normative words. But should such occasions arise, as they sometimes do, then we ought to be in a position to check on intuition by analysis, and this is precisely what is precluded by a sole reliance on the intuitive approach, be it either the naive form or its sophisticated phenomenological version; hence the need for correction by other approaches.

2. The phenomenological movement, originating with Edmund Husserl (1859–1938), is one of the most influential philosophical movements of the twentieth century. As in classic philosophy, of which phenomenology is in a sense a continuation, there is a vast divergence between individual phenomenologically oriented thinkers. The common bond which unites all phenomenologists is the stress laid upon the investigation of concrete phenomena, and the use of the phenomenological method by which to achieve this.

The phenomenological method applied to the investigation of concrete phenomena consists in these essential steps:

(1) Suspension of belief as to existence or non-existence of phenomena in order to avoid prejudging them.

(2) The grasp of phenomena by direct vision or intuition.

(3) The analytic examination and description of phenomena.

(4) Systematic explanation of phenomena and the ways in which they appear.

(5) Determining patterns or essences of particular phenomena.

(6) Apprehension of essential relationships among essences.

(7) Determining the way in which a phenomenon establishes itself in consciousness.[3]

The phenomenological method is thus broadly conceived. It can incorporate the methods of positivist analysis as well as ordinary language philosophy without losing its distinctive features.

Although phenomenological teachings and the opinions of phenomenologists on language are far from being as uniform as

---

[3]Herbert Spiegelberg, *The Phenomenological Movement* (The Hague: Martinus Nijhoff, 1960), II, 675f.

those of the analysts, there are a few basic attitudes that are common among them in regard to language. These attitudes consist in the stress on intuition and feeling in cognitive processes pertaining to language, and on the emotional content, symbols, and meaning in language.

It is not amiss at this juncture to point out that when judging in matters of law and morals in everyday life, men use what is called common sense—a compound of intuitive logic, feeling, and experience. This same common sense with a larger portion of experience is used by legislators, judges, practicing lawyers, and scholars. The phenomenological approach in law and morals, and in the language of law and morals, can thus be represented in a sense as an attempt to vindicate common sense in law and morals.

3. The problem of intuition is twofold: on the one hand there is the need for it in discovery and for the objective certainty that it gives, and on the other hand it is vague and sometimes erroneous, even in logic and mathematics, where there is the least chance for it to err undetected for long.

Intuitive knowledge in logic and mathematics is not invoked as some private experience or knowledge that cannot be ascertained by anyone with sufficient ability and acquaintance with these subjects. Moreover, we know by experience that intuition in logic and mathematics 'works.' Thus when we say that "$2 + 2 = 4$," or that "if $x < y$ and $y < z$ then $x < z$," we are intuitively certain that this is so and we expect everyone to be able to realize this fact for himself. Until recently these mathematical propositions were not only believed to be true, but to be incapable of further proof than intuitive evidence could offer. Now, although their truth is not doubted, they can be proved by strict deductive methods, provided certain assumptions are made. In these cases and in a vast number of other cases in logic and mathematics, we know that the conclusions reached intuitively can be proved by deductive methods and that our intuition was 'right.'

Once a discovery has been made, then many—though by no means all—of the statements in logic and mathematics can be demonstrated with no room for doubt or vagueness whatsoever. Intuition, however, was necessary to make the discovery even in these most exact sciences, and there are probably not many people who would make any issue of using intuition in logic and mathematics.

The situation is different, however, when we move out of these into other areas of human knowledge, and especially so when we move on the level of human existence in which moral and legal issues play a paramount role. In these areas deductive methods are seldom used and many times cannot be used.

There are two opposite positions that have been taken in regard to the use of intuition in morals and law and in normative discourse: the analytic and the intuitionist. The former categorically denies any value to intuition and feeling in legal and moral matters;[4] the latter categorically asserts its value in these matters. If the problem were differently stated, however, i.e., not, "What is the value of intuition vs. analytic methods," but, "How far can analytic methods, assuming that they are more accurate and certain, be used before we must resort to intuition," then many issues could be settled and sterile discussions and controversies eliminated.

4. Language has a structure which can be discerned by the feeling for the given language, and it has an internal logic of its own.[5] The artificial languages of symbolic logic and other formalized systems remain rooted in the natural language, and hence in this internal logic of the natural language.[6] The logic of the natural language is in turn rooted in intuition.[7] Natural language thus remains ultimately the metalanguage of any artificial systems.

Through intuitive understanding a community of minds and ends is established, and it is precisely for this reason that certain subjective and emotional contents can be communicated. Nor does communication of emotional and symbolic contents signify that the communicants do not know what they are talking about. "Intelligibility is not a privilege enjoyed only by logical assertions."[8] It is worthwhile to mention here that the religious, magic, or ideological systems which have served in every known culture as the backbone of the given culture, as well as of its legal and moral

---

[4]Cf. P. F. Strawson, "Ethical Intuitionism," *Readings in Ethical Theory*, ed. W. Sellars and J. Hospers (New York: Appleton-Century-Crofts, 1952), pp. 250–259, for analytic objections to intuitionism.

[5]Mikel Dufrenne, *Language and Philosophy*, pp. 34, 73.

[6]*Ibid.*, p. 88.

[7]*Ibid.*, pp. 67f.

[8]*Ibid.*, p. 84

system, largely consist of symbolic and emotive contents which are intelligible and logically consistent.

5. Natural language does not consist of propositions eternalized in a rigid system, but of components that can never be completely rendered by the system alone. Natural language does not have merely a horizontal dimension, as do artificial languages which consist of fixed signs, but a vertical dimension as well, which shows natural language in its growth, in the constant shifting of its sounds and meanings, in the addition of new elements and the elimination of outlived elements. This holds especially true of natural language in regard to law and morals.

There are permanent constituents in natural language and there are those that change. There are those that can be separated for the purposes of analysis and there are those that cannot. There are those that are accessible to discursive reasoning and there are those that are accessible, it at all, only to intuition and feeling.

Natural language has four kinds of components on the semantic level: the logical thread that permeates every natural language; the grammatical thread that permeates every given natural language; the reference contents that contain information about an object or individual, or a class of objects or individuals; and the emotive and symbolic elements through which feelings, attitudes, and emotions are communicated.

6. The common logical thread that permeates every natural language is not individually, socially, or culturally affected. It is partially by virtue of this common logic that sentences can be translated from one language into another. It is also partially by virtue of this common logic that a statement or discourse is judged to make sense or nonsense. The proper use of this common logic in every language represents the absolute minimum for meaningful communication.

Sentences are strung in the course of speech or writing into a more or less coherent utterance and then a discourse by the use of intuitive logic, and the usual way of checking the consistency of sentences in natural language is by common sense—a combination of intuitive logic, feeling, and experience.

The connection of sentences, as well as the elements within the sentences, depends also upon grammar. Grammar, which presupposes common logic, partially differentiates one group of languages from another and one language from others within the group of kindred languages. Here the analytic weapons of linguistic science can be successfully used to clarify the given language, although the mastery of the linguistic science of the given language need not necessarily make one a master of that language. This fact can be observed clearly in non-native speakers of the language who have mastered the grammar and the vocabulary sometimes better than native speakers, yet have not acquired what is colloquially called the "feel" for the language.

The grammatical aspects of natural language are socially, historically, and culturally conditioned, and hence no "direct" translation of these aspects from one language into another is possible, or even an exact rendering within the same language. At best more or less equivalent forms can be found, at least within the same family of languages.

7. The components of sentences consist of words. The important words for our purposes are stereotyped terms or formulas and their clusters. Formulas are especially common in religious, poetic, and normative language.

Terms are vehicles for reference contents within a sentence. They refer to concrete objects or individuals such as 'this chair,' 'this man,' or they apply to their classes, such as 'chair,' 'man,' and to abstract ideas and their classes, such as 'right,' 'tort,' 'murder,' 'good,' 'freedom,' etc. Terms with *concrete* referents need not be individually, socially, culturally or historically conditioned, and their translation from one language to another need not present difficulties. Terms having *abstract* referents are individually, socially, culturally, and historically conditioned, and present great difficulties to even intuitive understanding, let alone to semantic analysis. Hence their translation from one language to another is difficult, though not impossible in principle. Correspondingly, the semantic analysis of them is difficult but partially possible. However, the semantic analysis of terms of natural language cannot be conducted profitably if the diachronous dimension of language is ignored. But ultimately all of these means can at best be only supplementary to intuition and feeling for them and their meanings.

8. Terms are expressed by words in spoken language, which

in turn are represented by signs in written language. Signs are governed by definite syntactical rules as well as reference possibilities in any meaningful communication. Signs as such need not be associated with emotive and symbolic referents. Thus the signs '+' and '—', denoting certain mathematical operations, are not associated with emotive referents. Every sign, however, can become associated with emotive and symbolic referents, in which case the sign becomes a symbol. A symbol in turn may lose emotive and symbolic contents, in which case only the sign as the carrier of emotive and symbolic contents is left. Several examples of potentially an infinite number of signs and symbols will be given here, with, however, no exhaustive analysis of them.

(1) The word as well as the object 'cross' is to Christians a 'we' symbol or a symbol of belonging, dedication, and love. To Muslims and Jews it is a symbol of persecution, suffering, and hostility. To those who have never heard of Christianity it is a mere sign. To ex-Christians it is a symbol that has become a sign.

(2) The word 'death' is a biologically conditioned symbol. There are analytic ways of describing death, e.g., as 'the transformation of molecular structures within an object x.' But this analytic description does not and cannot render what 'death' means to human beings in human terms. Only a symbol fully charged emotionally can do it.

(3) The word 'murder' is a sign fully charged symbolically only within a certain religious, moral, and legal framework. Thus if a Muslim kills another Muslim it is considered 'murder' by Islamic law, and charged with all the emotive significance that goes with the word 'murder.' Should a Muslim kill a non-Muslim, the killing is not considered 'murder,' but a simple killing like the killing of an animal, or even a meritorious deed if he kills a recalcitrant enemy of Islam. The converse attitudes toward killing Muslims by Christians could be adduced. Although the analysis of the term 'murder' in terms of semantics and linguistics, as well as the legal, moral, and cultural frameworks, can clarify the term in these respects, no amount of analysis can render the emotive contents of horror, indignation, etc., with which the word 'murder' is charged.

Analogous considerations are possible for certain other types of killing, such as 'blood vengeance,' 'slaying the enemy,' and 'execution.'

(4) The words 'right' and 'freedom' are normative terms which are symbolically and emotively charged, in addition to having certain referents within the cultural framework of the West. Useless discussions and controversies about the 'meaning' of these and similar words are familiar enough. What is unfamiliar is the reason for them: that the emotive and symbolic significance of the terms cannot be determined by analytic means.

9. Although the emotive and symbolic referents of terms can neither be determined nor explained analytically, their scope can be delineated: e.g., the words 'hate' and 'love' can be applied meaningfully only to human beings, as in the sentences 'Peter hates Paul,' or 'Peter loves Clara.' 'Steel loves concrete,' or 'Steel hates concrete,' is meaningless unless the words be used metaphorically. It may also be pointed out here that 'love' and 'hate' are not incompatible terms because of any rules of formal logic, but because the emotive and symbolic referents are incompatible.

The emotive and symbolic referents can either be 'understood' by intuition and feeling or not understood at all. This 'understanding' is, however, conditioned biologically, individually, socially, culturally, and historically. Sexual symbols, for example, are conditioned biologically, although society and culture may mold their way of expression. Religious and ideological symbols can be conditioned by the religion and ideology of the given society.[9] For these reasons the emotive and symbolic associations of terms cannot be translated at all, just as esthetic, religious, or love experiences cannot be translated. At best, more or less analogous but not equivalent experiences can be evoked to aid the 'understanding' of symbolic associations.

10. The phenomenological approach broadly conceived is the least dogmatic of all approaches to normative discourse. Its strength lies in its ability to utilize the positive aspects of other methods. Its weakness lies in the always lurking possibility of relying too much

---

[9]Max Scheler, who introduced the phenomenological method into law and morals, and Nicolai Hartmann, who developed the most comprehensive system of ethics by means of the phenomenological method, both postulated that it is by the immediate intuition or feeling for 'values' that men judge what is 'justice,' 'injustice,' 'right,' 'wrong,' etc. Scheler and Hartmann rightly insisted upon the importance of intuitive insight and feeling in law and morals, but neglected to take into consideration the biological, personal, cultural, historical, and religio-ideological factors which may affect intuitive insight and feeling, and which are partially accessible to analytic methods of investigation.

on intuitive 'understanding,' with the consequent neglect to verify whenever possible by analytic methods. Clarification by analysis is desirable whenever possible, but beyond a certain point it is not only impossible but nonsensical.

The phenomenological approach is not different from the common-sense approach. It assumes that those who have better than average talents and experience in law and morals will also understand better the language of law and morals. It also assumes that the great systems of morals and law, created by the collective wisdom of ages, do not rest on endless ambiguities and misunderstandings of normative language, as some analysts would lead us to believe, but rather on sound understanding, which ought to be and is continually being corrected in the process of development and refinement of the language of law and morals.

III. *The Approach of Ordinary-Language Philosophy to Normative Discourse*

1. The most publicized philosophical movement in the English-speaking world at present is undoubtedly the movement referred to as "linguistic analysis," "Oxford philosophy," "analysis," "linguistic philosophy," or "ordinary-language philosophy." The movement took its basic idea—that the main task of philosophy is the clarification of language—from Ludwig Wittgenstein (1889–1951). This idea was then developed into a philosophical program by Gilbert Ryle, who also devised a technique by which to accomplish this program. This program was outlined by Ryle in terms of the following tasks to be accomplished by linguistic philosophy: (1) to determine whether or not the relation between grammatical and logical forms in given instances is proper;[10] (2) to discover in particular cases whether an expression is misleading or not;[11] (3) to seek out prevalent type of misleading expressions;[12] and (4) to restate more misleading expressions in terms of those less misleading, but with these provisos:

Philosophy must then involve the exercise of system-

---

[10]Gilbert Ryle, "Systematically Misleading Expressions," *Logic and Language*, ed. A. G. N. Flew (1st series; Oxford: Basil Blackwell, 1952), p. 34.

[11]*Ibid.*, p. 35.

[12]*Ibid.*

atic restatement. But this does not mean that it is a department of philology or literary criticism.

Its restatement is not the substitution of one noun for another or one verb for another. That is what lexicographers and translators excel in. Its restatements are transmutations of syntax controlled not by desire for elegance or stylistic correctness but by desire to exhibit the forms of the facts into which philosophy is the inquiry.

I conclude, then, that there is, after all, a sense in which we can properly inquire and even say "what it really means to say so and so." For we can ask what is the real form of the fact recorded when this is concealed or disguised and not duly exhibited by the expression in question. And we can often succeed in stating this fact in a new form of words which does exhibit what the other failed to exhibit. And I am for the present inclined to believe that this is what philosophical analysis is, and that this is the sole and whole function of philosophy.[13]

Ryle's program has been put into effect by a number of followers under whose influence such new concepts as 'the language of morals,'[14] 'the language of religion,' and 'the language of law' were introduced. The most important analysts in so far as the language of morals and law are concerned are J. L. Austin,[15] R. M. Hare,[16] P. Nowell-Smith,[17] and H. L. A. Hart.[18] Consideration of their work will give us an adequate idea of what ordinary-language philosophy can do for the language of law and morals.

2. H. L. A. Hart in *The Concept of Law*, his major analytical work, characterized it in the following way:

The lawyer will regard the book as an essay in analytical jurisprudence, for it is concerned with the clarification of the general framework of legal thought, rather than with the criticism of law or legal policy. Moreover, at many points, I have raised questions which may well be said to be about the meanings of words.[19]

---

[13]*Ibid.*, p. 36.

[14]An excellent discussion of ordinary language philosophy with respect to the language of morals is provided by Carl Wellman's *The Language of Ethics*.

[15]*How to Do Things with Words* (New York: Oxford University Press, 1950).

[16]*The Language of Morals* (Oxford: The Clarendon Press. 1961).

[17]*Ethics* (New York: Penguin Books, 1959).

[18]*The Concept of Law*.

[19]*Ibid.*, p. vii.

In these words Hart enunciates the scope of analysis' task in law, which is clearly within the scope of the program set up by Ryle.

Hart also maintains that ordinary-language analysis in law is simply the analytical jurisprudence of Austin, Kelsen, and others, improved through the new techniques of analysis due to advances in philosophy, and particularly in logic.[20] This is how the new technique would operate in practice:

> The technique I suggested was to forego the useless project of asking what the *words* taken alone stood for or meant and substitute for this a characterization of the function that such words performed when used in the operation of a legal system. This could be found at any rate in part by taking the characteristic sentences in which such appear in a legal system, e.g., in the case of the expression "a right," such a characteristic sentence as "x has a right to be paid y dollars." Then the elucidation of the concept was to be sought by investigating what were the standard conditions in which such a statement was true and in what sort of contents and for what purpose such statements were characteristically made. This would get us away from the cramping suggestion that the meaning of a legal word is to be found in some fact-situation with which it is correlated in some way as simple and straightforward as the way in which the word "chair" is correlated with a fact-situation and substitute for this an inquiry into the job done by such a word when the word is used in a legal system to do its standard task.[21]

Lastly it ought to be pointed out that Hart insists that the analytic approach is not the only one; his position on this issue is rather an exceptional one:

> Finally, it is, I hope, clear from all that I have said that I do not regard analytical jurisprudence as exclusive of other forms of jurisprudence. There is room, of course, for other approaches, although I have my own reasons for preferring the analytical as an educational tool. On the other hand, I think that no candid student of sociology could deny that, valuable as the insights have been which

---

[20]"Analytical Jurisprudence in Mid-twentieth Century: A Reply to Professor Bodenheimer," *University of Pennsylvania Law Review*, CV, No. 7 (1957), 960-974.
[21]*Ibid.*, p. 961.

it has provided, the average book written in the socio-logical vein, whether on legal topics or otherwise, is full of unanalyzed concepts and ambiguities of just that sort which a training in analysis might enable a student to con-front successfully. Both psychology and sociology are relatively young sciences with an unstable framework of concepts and a correspondingly uncertain and fluctuating terminology. If they are to be used to illuminate us as to the nature of law, these sciences must be handled with care and with a sensitivity to the types of ambiguity and vague-ness, and also other linguistic anomalies, which the student will best learn to appreciate in handling the leading con-cepts of the law in an analytical spirit.[22]

There is no more to be added in order to explain what Hart and the analysts consider to be the task of analysis.[23] It must only be pointed out that Hart's position, according to which ordinary-language analysis in law follows in the tradition established by Austin, Kelsen, and others, is not to be accepted without qualifica-tions, if at all.

3. The analysis of the language of morals has been carried much farther by outstanding analysts than has the analysis of the language of law. However, the analysis of the language of morals must coincide to a large extent with the respective analysis of the language of law, and indeed it has done just that in the treatises of outstanding analysts.

R. M. Hare was among the first to deal in depth with the lan-guage of morals from the ordinary-language-philosophy view-point.[24] Thereafter the subject was dealt with fully by P. Nowell-Smith,[25] and by others on a lesser scale.

---

[22]*Ibid.*, p. 974.

[23]To see Hart's analysis in action, the following works of his ought to be consulted: "The Ascription of Responsibility and Rights," *Logic and Language,* pp. 145–166; "Negligence, *Mens Rea* and Criminal Responsibility," *Oxford Essays in Jurisprudence,* ed. A. G. Guest (Oxford: The University Press, 1961), pp. 29–49.

[24]*The Language of Morals.* The language of morals first received full-scale scrutiny, though not from the ordinary-language-philosophy-view, by Charles L. Stevenson, as he correctly pointed out in his address, "Relativism and Non-Rela-tivism in the Theory of Value," American Philosophical Association, *Proceedings and Addresses, 1961–1962* (Yellow Springs, Ohio: Antioch College Press, 1963), pp. 32f.

[25]*Ethics.*

4. The contributions of ordinary-language philosophy to the study of normative discourse can be said to consist in the following:

(1) Drawing attention to the significance and use of normative language.

(2) Pointing to the semantic peculiarities of normative language in contradistinction to the conventional semantics of descriptive language.

(3) Finding a technique by which to lay bare semantic problems in connection with normative sentences, and to a certain extent with the component terms of normative as well as imperative sentences.

(4) Drawing attention to the importance of use and context in analysis of normative discourse.

(5) Pointing out that words of natural language, and hence of normative discourse, have an 'open texture,' which is to say that the boundaries of their referents are not definite but open.

The overall criticism of ordinary-language analysis of normative discourse can be directed against their attempt to reduce all of analysis of language, indeed all of philosophy, to one particular technique of investigation and one program.[26]

IV. *The Semantic Theory of Fodor and Katz*

1. The semantic theory that can serve for the analysis of sentences, and the only semantic theory developed on the basis of a thorough knowledge of the current work in linguistics, is the theory of Jerry A. Fodor and Jerrold J. Katz.[27] The Fodor-Katz theory is in principle very simple: given the intuitive understanding which a fluent speaker has in speaking and interpreting the sentences of

---

[26]A judicious criticism of ordinary-language philosophy from the standpoint of structural linguistics has been advanced by J. J. Katz, *Philosophy of Language;* and from the standpoint of jurisprudence by Jerome Hall, "Analytic Philosophy and Jurisprudence," *Ethics,* LXXVII, No. 1 (1966), 14–28.

[27]"The Structure of a Semantic Theory," *The Structure of Language* (Englewood Cliffs: Prentice Hall, 1965), pp. 479–518. Published previously in *Language,* XXXIX (1963), pp. 170–210. A shorter version of the theory with some applications is given by Jerrold J. Katz, "Analyticity and Contradiction in Natural Language," *The Structure of Language,* pp. 519–543. A non-technical presentation of the theory with application to the meaning of "good" is given by Jerrold J. Katz, "Semantic Theory and the Meaning of 'Good'," *The Journal of Philosophy,* LXI, No. 23 (1964), 739–766. Extensive and clearer treatment of the theory is offered in Katz's *The Philosophy of Language,* pp. 97–185.

his language, an adequate semantic theory ought to be able to supply the framework for a formal analysis and description of such an intuitive understanding.[28]

The job that a semantic theory has to accomplish is to take up the linguistic task in interpreting sentences where the grammar leaves off and carry it up to the point where the socio-physical setting determines the interpretation of the discourse or individual sentences.[29] The task of this semantic theory is conceived thus to consist in interpreting sentences in isolation from the socio-physical setting:[30]

> We thus arrive at the following conception of a semantic theory. The basic fact that a semantic theory must explain is that a fluent speaker can determine the meaning of a sentence in terms of the meanings of its constituent lexical items. To explain this fact a semantic theory must contain two components: a dictionary of the lexical items of the language and system of rules (which we shall call *projection rules*) which operate on full grammatical descriptions of sentences and on dictionary entries to produce semantic interpretations for every sentence of the language. Such a theory would explain how the speaker applies dictionary information to sentences and would thus solve the projection problem for semantics by reconstructing the speaker's ability to interpret any of the infinitely many sentences of his language. The central problem for such a theory is that a dictionary usually supplies more senses for a lexical item than it bears in an occurrence in a given sentence, for a dictionary entry is a characterization of every sense a lexical item can bear in any sentence. Thus, the effect of the projection rules must be to select the appropriate sense of each lexical item in a sentence in order to provide the correct readings for each distinct grammatical structure of that sentence. The semantic interpretations assigned by the projection rules operating on

---

[28]*The Structure of Language,* pp. 481ff.

[29]*Ibid.,* pp. 486-491.

[30]The Fodor-Katz semantic theory contrasts sharply here, and in our opinion to its disadvantage, with the ordinary-language philosophy that stresses linguistic context, as well as with Firthian views on semantics which stress the importance of socio-cultural context (J. R. Firth, *Papers in Linguistics* [London: Oxford University Press, 1964], pp. 7, 15, 16, 19, 27, 32, 181, 186, 187).

grammatical and dictionary information must account in the following ways for the speaker's ability to understand sentences: They must mark each semantic ambiguity a speaker can detect; they must explain the source of the speaker's intuitions of anomaly when a sentence evokes them; they must suitably relate sentences speakers know to be paraphrases of each other.

Pictured in this way, a semantic theory interprets the syntactic structure a grammatical description of a language reveals. This conception thus gives content to the notion that a semantic theory of a natural language is analogous to a model which interprets a formal system. Further, it explicates the exact sense of the doctrine that the meaning of a sentence is a function of the meanings of the parts of a sentence. The system of projection rules is just this function.[31]

The Fodor-Katz theory consists of two parts: (a) methods dealing with the formalization of dictionary entries; and (b) the projection rules. Fodor and Katz use the *Shorter Oxford* and the *Webster's New Collegiate* dictionaries to demonstrate how the formalization of the dictionary entries is to be accomplished. But in principle the method can be used on any dictionary, no matter how complex, so long as the number of entries is finite. Their projection rules assign the possibilities of readings from dictionary entries that can be adopted and dictionary entries that must be discarded for the sentence under consideration. The Fodor-Katz projection rules still need crystallization and maturation, but to a certain extent the theory can be useful for the semantic analysis of normative sentences, as we shall endeavor to show.

2. Formal analysis by means of the Fodor-Katz theory can be accomplished by employing either the tree form or the linear form of analysis. The tree form is the most perspicuous for short sentences,[32] while long sentences can be analyzed more easily by means of the linear form used by Katz.[33]

---

[31]Fodor and Katz, *The Structure of Language*, pp. 493f.
[32]*Ibid.*, p. 505.
[33]*Journal of Philosophy*, LXI, No. 23, 740.

We select as an example of analysis the arbitrary imperative sentence: 'You shall not kill.'[34] This normative sentence is intuitively clear to a fluent speaker of English, nor does it present any grammatical difficulties. The sentence in tree form appears this way:

Sentence

Pronoun

Verb phrase

YOU

Verb transitive

Adverb

Verb transitive

SHALL NOT

KILL

---

[34]Ex. 20 : 13, RSV. An objection might be raised against using the English translation rather than the Hebrew original of this sentence. The answer to this objection is that it is precisely the English translation of the sentence that interests us at the moment. Should we be interested in the Hebrew original the analysis could be performed in the same way.

These are the dictionary entries which are possibilities for the components of the sentence:[35]

(a) *You*, pron., ... the ordinary pronoun of the second person, ..., now used regularly as either objective or nominative, and with either plural or singular meaning, but always, when used as subject, taking a plural verb.

(b) *Shall*, v.t., ... 1. (used, generally, in the first person to indicate simple future time): ... 2. (used, generally, in the second and third persons, to indicate promise or determination): *You shall do it*. 3. (used interrogatively ...). 5. (used with the second or third persons, *shall* implies authority, command, threat, promise, determination, or inevitability): *Thou shalt not steal*.

(c) *Not*, adv., a word expressing negation, denial, refusal, or prohibition: *not far, you must not do that*.

(d) *Kill*, v.t., 1. to deprive (any living creature or thing) of life in any manner; cause the death of; slay. 2. to destroy; do away with; extinguish: *kill hope*. 3. to destroy or neutralize the active qualities of. 4. to spoil the effect of. 5. to get rid of (time) by some method (usually easy) of spending it. 6. to overcome completely or with irresistible effect. 7. to cancel (a word, paragraph, item, etc.). 8. to defeat or veto (a legislative bill, etc.). 9. *Elect.* to render (a circuit) dead. 10. *Lawn Tennis*, to hit (a ball) with such force that its return is impossible.—v.i., 11. to inflict or cause death. 12. to commit murder.

Instead of the Fodor-Katz projection rules, which suffer from a needless technical-language syndrome, we shall use the following rules in order to determine the possible interpretations of the sentence.

(1) A sentence is anomalous if no reading of dictionary entries can render a meaningful interpretation of it.

(2) A sentence is unambiguous if the dictionary entries make only one interpretation of it possible.

(3) A sentence is n-ways ambiguous if the dictionary entries make possible n-interpretations of it.

---

[35]*The American College Dictionary* (New York: Random House, 1951, 1969) is used for simplicity's sake. A more elaborate dictionary would be more precise but its entries would also be more complicated. The Fodor-Katz procedure of evaluating dictionary entries is also modified in order to simplify the analysis.

Testing by the first rule we find that there are some readings of the dictionary entries that make the interpretation of the sentence meaningful, which readings are:

(a) *You:* 1. Used as a second person singular.[36] 2. Used as a second person plural.[37]

(b) *Shall:* 1. Used generally in the second person to indicate promise or determination.[38] 2. Used with the second person to imply command.[39]

(c) *Not:* 1. Used to imply negation, prohibition.

(d) *Kill:* 1. Used in the sense to deprive of life, slay.

Applying the second rule on the sentence we find that it is not unambiguous. And applying the third rule we find that it is ambiguous in the following four ways:

(1) You_1 + $shall_1$ + not + kill.
(2) You_2 + $shall_1$ + not + kill.
(3) You_1 + $shall_2$ + not + kill.
(4) You_2 + $shall_2$ + not + kill.

The modified Fodor-Katz methods can take us only thus far in disambiguating the sentence 'You shall not kill.' To determine the meaning of the sentence further one must resort to extralinguistic means. In order to show exactly why semantic analysis alone cannot disambiguate this sentence completely we proceed to apply extralinguistic analysis.

We can first eliminate the interpretations based on you_1 by considering the literary and socio-cultural context of the writing wherein the sentence appears. In the light of the literary and socio-cultural context the sentence was addressed to a group of people. Hence you_1 is to be eliminated. It ought to be added, however, that this elimination of you_1 rests on intuitive insight and the general knowledge of the setting of the sentence, which cannot be formalized. But suppose that this intuitive insight is correct; then we are left with these possible interpretations:

(1) You_2 + $shall_1$ + not + kill.
(2) You_2 + $shall_2$ + not + kill.

---

[36]Abbreviated as you_1
[37]Abbreviated as you_2.
[38]Abbreviated as $shall_1$.
[39]Abbreviated as $shall_2$.

Relying again on contextual interpretation the following explanations of you_2 can be given.

(1) You_2 refers to a class of humans known as Israelites.

(2) You_2 refers to a class of Neo-Manicheans.

(3) You_2 refers to a class of humans known as Christians.

(4) You_2 refers to all humans.

Next, still relying on contextual interpretation, $shall_1$ can be
eliminated and $shall_2$ retained, since a command was intended.

And finally, these interpretations of the enthymematic *kill* can
be given:[40]

(1) *Kill* can refer to all living beings.

(2) *Kill* can refer to all humans.

(3) *Kill* can refer to a subclass of humans.

The medieval Neo-Manicheans considered that the enthymematic *kill* ought to be understood in the first sense. The traditional
theological interpretations considered that *kill* ought to be understood in the second sense, restricting even that interpretation to un-
justified killing, in other words to a subclass of humans. But for
the sake of simplicity let us overlook this restriction and consider
that the theological interpretation understands *kill* in the second
sense. The third sense was probably intended when this sentence
was formulated, since it was meant primarily to govern the conduct of the society within which the Decalogue grew. But again
for simplicity's sake, let us eliminate this sense since it was maintained neither for very long nor firmly and clearly.

These are the remaining interpretations of the sentence which
are irreducible by further analysis, and the decision which one to
accept and which ones to reject rests on theological considerations.

(1) You_2 (Israelites) + $shall_2$ + not + kill (human beings).

(2) You_2 (Christians) + $shall_2$ + not + kill (human beings).

(3) You_2 (Neo-Manicheans) + $shall_2$ + not + kill (any living beings).

(4) You_2 (all human beings) + $shall_2$ + not + kill (any living beings).

(5) You_2 (all human beings) + $shall_2$ + not + kill (human
beings).

---

[40] I am indebted here to Carl Wellman.

This completes the formal analysis of the sentence, 'You shall not kill.' A simple example was chosen intentionally in order to exhibit clearly how the method works and what it can yield. The method works in the same way for complicated sentences, except that the analyses are more involved.

In order to make this formal analysis, certain assumptions had to be made, and these should be stated.[41]

(a) It was assumed that the dictionary entries themselves were correct. This assumption could be challenged, since the dictionary entries are made intuitively by lexicographers on the basis of their knowledge of the language, the uses of words, and the socio-cultural context. However, no general formal method of doing this is known, nor is it likely that one will be developed.

(b) It was further assumed that the dictionary entries contain a closed number of meanings for given words, which is not quite a correct assumption, since a natural language is in a process of constant development which ceases only by its becoming a dead language. However, this inaccuracy does not affect significantly the interpretation of the sentences of a given natural language, at least not for practical purposes. (This same assumption is made in applying the methods of formal logic for the purposes of analysis of the natural language.)

(c) It was also assumed that the meanings in terms of which the dictionary entries were explained are known, an assumption that can never be completely justified from the formal point of view in the case of the natural language.

(d) Lastly, it was assumed that the selection of meanings and the application of rules for the selection of meanings can be made correctly by direct inferences drawn intuitively.

This is what was achieved in the partial formal analysis of the sentence: The various possible meanings were surveyed and the appropriate possibilities singled out. This is done intuitively daily by fluent communicants in a natural language and in most cases is done correctly. The partial formalization of sentences as made above can verify and correct the intuition when necessary, and what is perhaps more important, make the intuitive grasp of the sentence precise and definite. Moreover, it can suggest new or overlooked

---

[41]These assumptions have not been made explicit by either Fodor or Katz.

interpretations of a sentence.[42] The situation here is quite analogous to the use of the measuring rod to verify and make precise the intuitive appraisal of the length of a plank. Thus the achievement of the partial formal analysis of sentences is quite modest, yet very significant for the sharpening of our understanding of normative discourse.

V. *Denotational Semantics*

1. Sentential components in terms of traditional grammar are the following grammatical forms: nouns, pronouns, adjectives, verbs, adverbs, prepositions, conjunctions, and interjections. All of these grammatical forms can enter as components of singular and general terms; but only nouns, verbs, and adjectives can appear independently as terms.[43] And also only nouns, verbs, adjectives, and adverbs, individually or in combination, can express normative contents independently.

We approached nouns, adjectives, verbs, and adverbs in the sentential analysis through the dictionary entries, assuming that the readings in the dictionary entries were correct and intelligible. This assumption, which was adequate for the sentential analysis, must now be examined and a deeper analysis of nouns, adjectives, verbs, and adverbs undertaken which will lead us beyond the linguistic to non-linguistic frameworks.

2. The convenient point of departure in the analysis of grammatical forms is to take them as the constants of a given natural language. The possibilities of solving the problem of meaning for these constants are the following:

(a) Finding equivalents of unknown constants in the given language which are known.

(b) Describing unknown constants in terms of other constants.

(c) Using extralinguistic means to determine the meaning of unknown constants.

The possibility of (a) as a solution must be eliminated, however, since the word problem for semi-groups, i.e., finding an al-

---

[42]I am indebted here to Carl Wellman.

[43]At this point we abandon the Fodor-Katz semantic theory, which proceeds in a different direction, and return to the semantic analysis of singular and general terms of natural language as the basic units of our analysis.

gorithm for deciding for any given alphabet and dictionary whether any two words in them are equivalent, is insoluble.[44]

The possibility of (b), solving the problem of meaning by resorting to the description of a constant, must ultimately be ruled out since the description of any constant is made in terms of others and is bound to be circular.

The only possibility of a solution left is (c), using extralinguistic means, i.e., by transcending the linguistic frameworks. Such a possibility will be explored in the continuation of our analysis.

3.. Denotational semantics, initiated by Frege for purposes of logical analysis of individual expressions and propositions and carried on by his successors,[45] has recently been utilized by linguists for purposes of solving the problem of meaning for morphemes.[46] This morphemic theory of meaning can most profitably be applied in the analysis of normative components of sentences, and indeed, with suitable additions and modifications it can offer in a sense a solution of the problem of meaning for normative concepts.

The morphemic theory distinguishes first between linguistic forms and the objects which they denote:

> The semantic continuum cannot be anything else but the real world, accessible to our senses. Parts of it, when referred to by means of a linguistic form, are usually called "things meant." The meaning of a linguistic form (morpheme or word) is its ability to point to (to denote) a number of things in reality. It is not to be identified with the "things meant," but it certainly can be defined in terms of them.[47]

---

[44]Stephen Cole Kleene, *Introduction to Metamathematics* (New York: D. Van Nostrand Co., 1952), pp. 382f.

[45]The significant contributions include: Gottlob Frege, "On Sense and Reference," *Translations from Philosophical Writings of Gottlob Frege*, ed. Peter Geach and Max Black (Oxford: Basil Blackwell, 1952); Alonzo Church, "The Need for Abstract Entities in Semantic Analysis," *Proceedings of the American Academy of Arts and Sciences*, LXXX, No. 1 (1951), 100–112; C. I. Lewis, "The Modes of Meaning," *Philosophy and Phenomenological Research*, IV (1943–44), Charles W. Morris, *Foundations of the Theory of Signs* (Chicago: The University of Chicago Press, 1960); Carnap, *Meaning and Necessity;* and Quine, *Word and Object.*

[46]The relevant works are: C. L. Ebeling, *Linguistic Units* ('S-Gravenhage: Mouton and Co., 1960); Laszlo Antal, *Questions of Meaning* (The Hague: Mouton and Co., 1963).

[47]Ebeling, *Linguistic Units*, p. 88.

This statement, naive though it may be from the philosophical viewpoint, is in substance correct. We can indeed clearly distinguish between the linguistic forms and "things meant." The following components of the meaning situation then emerge: (a) the linguistic form or sign; (b) the sense of the linguistic form; (c) the thing or object or entity meant or referred to which is called the denotatum or designatum or referent; and (d) the rule of reference or denotation or usage that governs the correct application of the linguistic form to the referent.[48] And by "meaning" we shall understand the result of the application of the rule of usage to the sign and the referent, i.e., this whole semantic complex.[49]

The following questions will have to be raised in connection with the morphemic theory of meaning:[50]

(a) The question of correspondence of sense with referent.

(b) The question of "concrete" vs. "abstract" words.

(c) The question of the emotive significance of words.

(d) The question concerning the establishment of the rule of usage.

(e) The question of ontological frameworks.

(a) The theory leaves the possibility open that a single morpheme may have one, two, or more senses correspond to no referent, a single referent, or a number of referents, and conversely, that one, two, or more referents may have a single sign correspond to them.[51] The decision as to which sense ought to be matched to which referent (if any) is then a matter for the rule of usage and contextual determination.

(b) The difference between "abstract" and "concrete" words is not the difference between the words but between the referents.

The difference which, according to Ullmann, exists between "cheval" and "liberté" is not the difference between the two concepts but the difference between the objects belonging to the two concepts. Thus, the "concrete concept" and the "abstract concept" are very unfortunate

---

48Morris, *Foundations*, pp. 5, 47; Antal, *Questions*, pp. 25f.

49Antal, the chief exponent of the morphemic theory of meaning, calls "meaning" what we termed "the rule of usage or reference or denotation." *Ibid.*

50The "morphemic theory of meaning" is not the name given to it by structural linguists. It has been introduced here to distinguish it from the theory originating with Frege and constructed for different purposes.

51Antal, *Questions*, pp. 30f.

terms, as they relate to a qualitative difference between concepts, although this difference does not exist in the quality of the concepts but only in the quality of the objects belonging to these concepts.[52]

And further:

As regards "concrete" and "abstract" meaning, we can only repeat that all meanings are abstract, since they are all rules, and that the difference alleged between "concrete" meaning and "abstract" meaning does not exist in the meanings but in the denotata. The meaning of "cheval" is as abstract as the meaning of "liberté," as both are only rules stating for what purpose we can use the sign "cheval" and the sign "liberté," respectively. At the same time, the denotatum of "cheval," i.e., the actual horse, and the denotatum of "liberté," i.e., actual liberty, differ as to their degree of concreteness.[53]

Moreover, the theory also shifts the problem of "vagueness of meaning" onto the referents.

We would not like to deal with the "vagueness" and "uncertainty" of meaning. For those of us who consider the meaning to be the rule of sign usage, it is quite obvious that the meaning is constant and fixed but that the denotatum is changeable and, in this sense, uncertain. (Of course, when we assert the permanence of meaning, we do not want to state that meaning is everlasting. From the standpoint of a synchronic condition, we consider it permanent within the framework of a given period.[54]

(c) The question of the emotive significance of words, especially those expressing normative contents, has been raised by the emotive theory of meaning.[55] Now whereas some normative words such as 'adjudication' do not ordinarily appear to carry emotional contents, some other normative words such as 'murder' do seem as a rule to carry emotional contents of strong disapproval. It is such normative words as 'duty,' 'murder,' etc., which are singled out and called "emotive" by the emotive theorists.

[52]*Ibid.*, p. 33.
[53]*Ibid.* "Meaning" is meant in our sense of the "rule of usage."
[54]*Ibid.*, p. 34.
[55]A. J. Ayer, *Language, Truth and Logic* (London: Gollancz, 1936, 1946). Ayer was the first to name normative concepts "emotive." The emotive theory of meaning with respect to normative concepts was developed by Charles S. Stevenson, *Ethics and Language* (New Haven: Yale University Press, 1944).

The question now arises as to whether it is the linguistic sign as such that carries emotional contents or its referent. At first glance it seems that it is the linguistic sign that carries the emotional contents, and hence the emotivists might be correct in calling such signs "emotive words." But when we reflect that to a person not knowing English the emotive contrast exhibited by such words as 'love' and 'hate' or 'justice' and 'injustice' is not noticeable, a different picture appears. Moreover, the emotive significance of the referent of 'murder' can be grasped without grasping the linguistic significance of the word 'murder,' whereas the converse is not the case. If the emotive word acted alone as a psychological stimulus, apart from the linguistic and social context, it should be able to evoke an emotional response the way a referent such as the scene of a murder does, which does not presuppose the linguistic communication of the English word 'murder.'[56] We conclude therefore that the emotive theory can be applied toward the solution of the problem of meaning of normative words provided that the referent be considered as the primary carrier of emotive contents and the sign as the carrier only in association with the referent and within the proper linguistic and socio-cultural context.

(d) The problem of establishing the rule of usage for a linguistic sign amounts to finding out: (a) which sign or signs correspond to which sense or senses; and (b) which sense or senses correspond to which referent or referents. A fluent speaker of the language establishes these correspondences intuitively every time he uses a word. The problem has been dealt with traditionally by philology, usually on the basis of linguistic context and sometimes also on the basis of socio-cultural context. And in very recent times ordinary-language philosophy has dealt with the problem, sometimes in a provocative manner but sometimes also in an amateurish fashion.

Both general linguistics and ordinary-language philosophy use intuition in establishing the usage of a given word, and in the final analysis intuition is crucial as far as the natural language is concerned.[57]

Usually the methods of general linguistics can be used, and oc-

---

[56] I am indebted here to Profs. Antony Oldknow and Carl Wellman.
[57] I am indebted here to Prof. Antony Oldknow.

casionally even those of ordinary-language philosophy, to establish the rule of usage for a given word. However, it must be stressed that these methods rest ultimately on intuition. It ought also to be added that for certain restricted purposes the rule of usage can be fixed by stipulation, as is sometimes done in law and scientific discourse.

(e) The question of ontological frameworks is the most important of them all. Rudolf Carnap realized this partially when he wrote:

> Generally speaking, if someone accepts a framework for a certain kind of entities, then he is bound to admit the entities as possible designata. Thus, the question of the admissibility of entities of a certain type or of abstract entities in general as designata is reduced to the question of the acceptability of the linguistic framework for those entities. Both the nominalistic critics, who refuse the status of designators or names to expressions like "red," "five," etc., because they deny the existence of abstract entities, and the skeptics, who express doubts concerning the existence and demand evidence for it, treat the question of existence as a theoretical question; the affirmative answer to *this* question is analytic and trivial and too obvious for doubt or denial, as we have seen. Their doubts refer rather to the system of entities itself; hence they mean the external question. They believe that only after making sure that there really is a system of entities of the kind in question are we justified in accepting the framework by incorporating the linguistic forms into our language. However, we have seen that the external question is not a theoretical question but rather the practical question whether or not to accept those linguistic forms. This acceptance is not in need of a theoretical justification (except with respect to expediency and fruitfulness), because it does not imply a belief or assertion. Ryle says that the "Fido"—Fido principle is "a grotesque theory." Grotesque or not Ryle is wrong in calling it a theory. It is rather the practical decision to accept certain frameworks. Maybe Ryle is historically right with respect to those whom he mentions as previous representatives of the principle, viz., John Stuart Mill, Frege, and Russell. If these prilosophers regarded the acceptance of a system of entities as a theory,

an assertion, they were victims of the same old, meta-physical confusion. But it is certainly wrong to regard *my* semantical method as involving a belief in the reality of abstract entities, since I reject a thesis of this kind as a metaphysical pseudo-statement.[58]

Carnap might have been able to escape the vicious circle of linguistic frameworks in which he had been making rounds but for his antimetaphysical bias.

The realm of referents is the realm of ontological entities ar-ranged into frameworks, which arrangement is conditioned by per-sonal and collective beliefs, attitudes, and experience. Thus, it is ultimately ontology that determines the meaning of linguistic forms in the sense that it determines, adequately or inadequately, the ref-erents.

The realm of referents may be well or poorly arranged, de-pending on the wish or ability to systematize or not the given ref-erents. This question belongs, however, to the province of ontology. What interests us in this connection is that natural language as such presupposes a certain arrangement, vague though it may be, of the referents into certain frameworks. Such frameworks are for example the framework of inanimate physical objects, the biological frame-work of animate objects, the framework of religious referents, the framework of esthetic referents, the framework of normative ref-erents, and others.

A dictionary entry explains a given word by adducing ex-planatory words for it which are from the same ontological frame-work, and this is the fact that makes dictionary entries circular. And when a broader explanation is desirable or necessary, a dictionary entry indicates it by adducing explanatory words for a given word from a more inclusive ontological framework, i.e., the ontological framework that includes the framework of the referent of the word to be explained. The explanation ultimately depends on the ability to grasp the referent and the ontological framework that the speaker intended.

These findings enable us now to formulate the general rule by means of which it can be decided when a given word is a nor-

---

[58]Rudolf Carnap, "Empiricism, Semantics, and Ontology," in his *Meaning and Necessity.*

mative word and when it is not:[59] *A word from a natural language is used normatively if and only if its referent belongs to a normative framework and cannot be determined otherwise than by an appeal to the given normative framework.*

Three classes of words can be distinguished as a consequence of the application of this rule:

(1) The class of purely normative words all of whose referents belong to the normative framework.

(2) The class of words some of whose referents are normative and some non-normative. The determination of the normative or non-normative referents respectively is made in such a case on the basis of context.

(3) The class of non-normative words all of whose referents are non-normative.

4. We proceed now to apply the denotational semantics as set forth above on arbitrarily chosen nouns, verbs, adjectives, and adverbs, the normatively significant traditional grammatical forms.

A. *Nouns.*

(1) *Adjudication*,[60] n. 1. act of adjudicating. 2. *Law.* (a) act of a court in making an order, judgment, or decree. (b) a judicial decision or sentence.

The meaning of the noun 'adjudication' is intuitively clear in the dictionary entry as well as in its sentential context. Moreover, every selection in the dictionary entry signifies an entity to which the word correctly applies. We have thus the linguistic sign which is the word 'adjudication,' its sense, and the entity or referent to which the word correctly applies. And the rule of usage was fixed by the dictionary compilers when they correlated the linguistic sign with its sense and its referent.

Ostensibly there should be no more complications with this word than with the word 'desk,' for example, which also is a linguistic sign, has a sense and a referent, namely the object of experience called 'desk.' In order to make the word 'desk' intelligible,

---

[59]As we have said earlier, this determination is made by jurists and moral philosophers intuitively. Our specification explicates, sharpens, and systematizes this intuitive determination.

[60]Let the sentential context for this noun be "The Opinion on Legislative Apportionment expressed for the majority by Chief Justice Earl Warren." *The New York Times,* June 16, 1964, pp. 23–30.

we have only to presuppose that the listener has had or is capable of having a direct or an indirect experience of the referent. No other presuppositions are necessary and no circularity within the linguistic framework need be involved.

Now when we compare the word 'desk' with the word 'adjudication,' we realize that more than the experience with physical objects is involved in the case of the latter. Thus should we presuppose only the experience with physical objects and take a person to a law court, all he could observe would be a certain behavior on the part of the people assembled there, which observation would be inadequate to understand the word 'adjudication' in that particular instance. *In order to understand it this person would have to be acquainted with the normative framework that is presupposed by the word, and only within which its meaning can be determined.* The difficulties in understanding the word 'adjudication' do not abide with the linguistic sign or its sense but in the referent, which cannot be even vaguely intimated without presupposing the normative framework.

(2) *Adultery*,[61] n. voluntary sexual intercourse between a married person and any other than the lawful spouse.

The entry explanation of the word is intuitively clear; which when broken down into its component elements is as follows: voluntary + sexual + intercourse + between + a + married + person + and + any + other + than + the + lawful + spouse.

Of these components the noun 'intercourse' together with its modifier 'sexual' presupposes the biological framework and the common experience that goes with it. However, the referent of 'adultery' is not sexual intercourse as such but a certain subclass of sexual intercourse specified by the normative framework of the given society. Without the normative framework there is no such thing as 'adultery,' but only sexual intercourse; nor are there such entities as 'married person' and 'lawful spouse' outside the normative framework. In addition to these the word 'voluntary,' although psychological in nature, plays here the role of further specifying the normative conditions under which sexual intercourse is to be considered 'adultery.'

Here also we have all the components of the meaning relation:

---

[61]Let the sentential context for this noun be Ex. 20 : 14.

the linguistic sign 'adultery,' its sense, the referent, and the rule of usage correlating the linguistic sign and its sense with the referent. The referent in turn is determined by the normative framework which presupposes the biological framework.

(3) *Crime*,[62] n. 1. an act committed or an omission of duty, injurious to the public welfare, for which punishment is prescribed by law, imposed in a judicial proceeding usually brought in the name of the state. 2. serious violation of human law: *steeped in crime*. 3. any offense, esp. one of grave character. 4. serious wrong-doing; sin. 5. *Colloq*. a foolish or senseless act; *it's* a crime to have to work so hard.

The referent of the word except for entry number 5 is explained entirely within the normative framework. Moreover, without a given normative framework no such thing as crime exists.

(4) *Justice*,[63] n. 1. the quality of being just; righteousness, equitableness, or moral rightness: *to uphold the justice of a cause*. 2. rightfulness or lawfulness, as a claim or title; justness of ground or reason: *to complain with justice*. 3. the moral principle determining just conduct. 4. conformity to this principle as manifested in conduct; just conduct, dealing, or treatment. 5. the requital of desert as by punishment or reward. 6. the maintenance or administration of law, as in judicial or other proceedings: *a court of justice*. 7. judgment of persons or causes by judicial process: *to administer justice in a community*. 8. a judicial officer; a judge or magistrate. 9. *do justice*, (a) to render or concede what is due to (a person or thing, merits, good intentions, etc.); treat or judge fairly. (b) to exhibit (oneself) in a just light, as in doing something: *the speaker hardly did justice to himself this evening*. (c) to show just appreciation of (something) by action: *to do justice to a good dinner by eating heartily*.

All of the entry selections except 9 (b) and (c) give the referents within the normative framework, and even they can be explained as idiomatic extensions of the normative word 'justice' which can certainly be eliminated contextually. The referent of the word

---

[62]Let the sentential context for this word be Amendment V to the Constitution of the United States.

[63]Let the sentential context of the word be the Preamble to the Constitution of the United States.

'justice' can therefore be determined only within the normative framework.

The word 'justice' is considered to be one of the most difficult normative words, perhaps the most difficult. In many cases it was thought to be a semantic problem to determine the meaning of 'justice'. This is true only up to a point, as was shown by our analysis, which solves the semantic problem, but the ontological problem still remains.[64]

B. *Verbs.*

(1) Deprive,[65] v.t. 1. to divest of something possessed or enjoyed; dispossess; strip; bereave. 2. to keep (a person, etc.) from possessing or enjoying something withheld.

The referents under the entry selections of this word are all determinable outside the normative framework. Hence, the word is non-normative.

(2) *Honor,*[66] v.t. 1. to hold in honor or high respect; revere. 2. to treat with honor. 3. to confer honor or distinction upon. 4. to worship (the Supreme Being). 5. to show a courteous regard for: *to honor an invitation.* 6. *Com.* to accept and pay (a draft, etc.) when due.

The referents of the entry selections can be determined only within a normative framework. Hence, the word is normative.

C. *Adjectives and Adverbs.*

The function of adjectives and adverbs is to serve as modifiers of nouns and verbs respectively. As such they do not denote independently, but in conjunction with nouns or verbs. Still the general rule governing normative words holds for them also, namely that a normative adjective or adverb can be determined only with the aid of normative words: nouns, verbs, adjectives, and adverbs, as the case may be.

---

[64]We cannot go into this problem here, but will merely point out that profound discussions of it are given by Plato in his *Republic,* by Aristotle in his *Nicomachean Ethics,* by Nicolai Hartmann in his *Ethik,* and by C. Perelman in his "De la Justice."

[65]Let the sentential context of this word be Amendment V to the Constitution of the United States.

[66]Let the sentential context of this word be Deut. 5 : 16.

(1) *Criminal,*[67] adj. 1. of or pertaining to crime or its punishment: *criminal law.* 2. of the nature of or involving crime. 3. guilty of crime.

The meaning of this word can be determined only with the help of normative nouns.

(2) *Just,*[68] adj. 1. actuated by truth, justice, and lack of bias: *to be just in one's dealings.* 2. in accordance with true principles; equitable; evenhanded: *a just award.* 3. based on right; rightful, lawful: *a just claim.* 4. agreeable to truth or fact; true; correct: *a just statement.* 5. given or awarded rightly, or deserved, as a sentence, punishment, reward, etc. 6. in accordance with standards, or requirements; proper, or right: *just proportions.* 7. righteous (esp. in Biblical use). 8. actual, real, or true.

The word is determinable only in terms of normative words, counting 'true' as a normative word, as indeed we must in these entry selections.

(3) *Justly,* adv. 1. in a just manner; honestly; fairly. 2. in conformity to fact or rule; accurately.

This is a normative word since its meaning is determinable entirely in terms of normative words.

D. *Compound Normative Expressions.*

The meaning of a compound normative expression is a function of its components. If a compound expression is to be normative then it must have at least one normative component and a maximum of all.

(1) one normative component: 'Human + rights' (adjective + noun).

(2) All normative components: 'Infamous + crime' (adjective + noun).[69]

5. The inquiry into the possibilities of semantic analysis of normative discourse is now completed. The semantic analysis as it was exemplified in the foregoing pages was mostly non-formal. Its formal completion is represented by logical analysis, which, if it is

---

[67]Let the sentential context of this word be Amendment V to the Constitution of the United States.

[68]Let the sentential context of this word be Amendment V to the Constitution of the United States.

[69]Let the sentential context for these be "The Opinion on Legislative Apportionment... by Chief Justice Warren"; and Amendment V to the Constitution of the United States.

to be used for concrete applications, presupposes semantic analysis. The job of semantic analysis is the clarification of sentences and their components. The job of logical analysis of normative discourse is the uncovering of its logical structure. The two kinds of analyses are thus not mutually exclusive, but supplementary.

The application of semantic analysis can be made in these realms:

(1) The realm of interpreting words and sentences as it is done in everyday life and in the law courts.

(2) The realm of empirical research into morals and law, which we shall refer to as descriptive ethics and jurisprudence.

(3) The realm of theoretical development of normative concepts as it is done in speculative or normative ethics and philosophy of law.

In all of these the determination of normative concepts is of fundamental importance. Normative concepts represent the determination of normative referents. Normative concepts are expressed by normative words and their combinations in ordinary language.

The concern with normative concepts can first be the investigation of normative concepts of a given normative system. Such investigations are preoccupations of descriptive ethics and jurisprudence. What the normative concepts of a given normative system are is determined intuitively in practice on the basis of experience with the given normative system and its socio-cultural context.[70] We are in a position now to check on this intuitive and experiential picking-out of normative words by means of the foregoing semantic analysis of normative discourse and the rule governing normative words.

The concern with normative concepts can secondly be the determination of normative concepts *in abstracto* as performed in normative ethics and philosophy of law. Whereas the determination of normative concepts for a given normative system is subject to empirical investigation and verification, the determination of normative concepts in normative ethics and philosophy of law generally is not, except that certain logical consequences can be drawn from such concepts, and except that certain empirical results can

---

[70]A systematic treatment of normative concepts of a selected normative system is exemplified in: Jovan Brkić, *Moral Concepts in Traditional Serbian Epic Poetry*.

be anticipated should such and such normative concepts be accepted and their realization be attempted.

The analysis of normative discourse leads us thus on the one hand into descriptive ethics and jurisprudence, and on the other hand into normative ethics and philosophy of law.

VI. *The Ontology of Normative Concepts*

1. It has already been mentioned that the convenient point of departure in the analysis of normative discourse is to treat traditional grammatical forms of natural language as constants. Of these some can have reference to non-linguistic entities independently and some only in conjunction with others. The grammatical forms that can have reference independently are nouns, verbs, and adjectives. The remaining traditional grammatical forms have non-referential linguistic functions and can be used referentially only in conjunction with nouns, verbs, and adjectives. In other words, only those grammatical forms that can independently serve as logical terms can also independently have reference. And it is precisely through the ability of terms to refer to non-linguistic entities that language can be used to communicate about non-linguistic phenomena. It is also precisely for this reason that language plays such an enourmous role in science and everyday life.

2. It was shown previously that the problem of meaning presents no insurmountable difficulties in so far as the sense of linguistic expressions and the rules of their usage are concerned. But the problem of meaning presents tremendous difficulties in so far as the determination of referents is concerned. And since the problem of meaning shifts thus from logic and linguistics into ontology, its solution will depend on ontological solutions.[71] And, we hasten to add, no generally acceptable solution to the ontological problem of reference has yet been offered.

3. The classification of terms into singular and general enters intuitively into any language wherein unique and divided reference is implicit. There is also another ontologically important classifica-

---

[71] The significance of ordinary-language philosophy consists in our opinion primarily in the airing and clarification of ontological issues in connection with natural language, and only secondarily if at all in the clarification of purely logical and semantic issues.

tion of terms which brings forth clearly the issues that are at stake in the problem of reference: that is the cross-classification of terms into concrete and abstract.[72] This nomenclature is not correct, since all terms are abstract, but what is correct is that their reference can be to concrete or abstract objects. Thus singular terms may purport to refer to unique concrete or abstract objects such as 'New York City' or 'o.' And general terms may be true of classes of concrete or abstract objects such as 'tree' or 'integers.'

4. It was shown previously that linguistic expressions cannot be described without circularity; as is the standard practice in composing dictionaries, wherein one entry is explained by means of other entries. And though this is true, it may appear somewhat odd, since in explaining a previously unknown word by description we seem to be doing something more than just replacing one unkonwn linguistic expression by others, ultimately equally unknown. But the oddness disappears as soon as it is realized that more is being done in such descriptions than just the describing of one unknown linguistic expression by others. Thus what the dictionary entries attempt to describe is not just the linguistic expressions but their functions within sentences, if they are non-referring linguistic expressions, or their referents, if they are referring linguistic expressions. And even so, what is actually being done is not an accurate description of functions or referents of linguistic expressions, but rather an attempt to determine the function or referents of linguistic expressions.

5. We shall leave aside the issue of determination of the function of non-referring linguistic expressions, since that is the province of linguistics, and concentrate on the problem of determination of reference for referring linguistic expressions.[73]

The determination of reference where referents are concrete objects proceeds in everyday life by means of intuition and sensual experience. Thus is determined, for instance, the referent of the

<hr>

[72]Quine, *Methods of Logic*, pp. 204f.

[73]Alfred Schutz, a phenomenologically oriented philosopher and social scientist, introduced the term 'typification' to designate for the social sciences what is intended here by the term 'determination.' We shall use the term 'determination' since it suits better our treatment of these problems. For Schutz's contribution to the problem of determination in the social sciences, cf. Jovan Brkić, "Methodological Problems of Sociology" *Sociologia Internationalis*, *VI*, No. 1 (1968), pp. 105-110.

singular term 'this desk' or the class of referents for the general term 'desk.' Since sensual experience is vague, so must be the determination of reference by means of it. Should a more precise determination of concrete referents be necessary, scientific instruments can be used to effect such a determination, but even so, no determination of concrete referents can be made absolutely precise, though sufficiently precise for the purposes of everyday life and the sciences in question. Nor is it possible to offer a general solution for the problem of determination of concrete referents, but only solutions for particular cases. If such a general solution were effected, it would represent a giant step toward a unified theory of nature. All the same, enormous strides in developing the sciences of nature have been made through such determinations; and we shall endeavor to show that analogous methods of determination can be applied to normative referents.

6. The determination of reference when referents are abstract entities is in some cases easier than when referents are concrete objects. In most cases it is very difficult and sometimes even virtually impossible.

The determination of reference for mathematical referents, which are all abstract, is completely soluble, if a Platonistic point of view is accepted, as is usual in mathematics. And even from the intuitionistic point of view the problem of reference in mathematics has a general solution for large classes of mathematical referents. We may conclude that only in mathematics is there a general solution for all practical purposes of the problem of reference.

7. The problem of reference for terms such as 'beauty,' 'nation,' 'society,' 'attitude,' 'mind,' 'ghost,' 'unicorn,' 'intelligence,' 'honor,' etc, is not soluble in the sense that clear-cut referents can be pointed out and associated with the sense of these terms. Intuitively, of course, communicants in a natural language such as English assume that they "know what they are talking about when using these terms, but a deeper analysis usually reveals that such "knowledge" is by no means certain and clear, and moreover that a reasonable doubt can be entertained as to whether such referents can be exhibited at all. And hence sterile disputes about the "meaning" of such terms oftentimes result.

But although a general solution of the problem of reference

for non-mathematical abstract referents is not feasible, a solution—
within limits—for such individual abstract referents and their
classes is in our opinion possible.

We envisage such a solution to proceed in the following steps:
(a) Intuitive grasp of the referent.
(b) Verification by the analysis of usage that the intuitive
mode of grasping the referent is not restricted to an individual, but
is universal in that language community (the method used by linguists).
(c) Contrasting the intuitive grasp of such a referent with
others in order to distinguish it from them in terms of similarity and
dissimilarity.
(d) Assigning the referent to a class and framework of similar
referents.
(e) Specification of the referent by descriptions as precise and
accurate as the problem at hand requires. (This is, in our interpretation, what is in fact proposed by the ordinary-language-philosophy
approach to meaning.) In empirical sciences this will be determined
by physical, biological, and socio-cultural context. In normative
ethics and philosophy of law it can further be made more precise
by stipulation, as is customary in law.

The very process of determining referents arranges them into
certain classes, frameworks, and order, as was clearly recognized
in classic ontology, which ordered entities in terms of lower and
higher ones. We shall refuse to commit ourselves initially to a hier-
archical ordering of classes and frameworks, and will introduce the
neutral term 'referential framework' as a class of classes of referents.
Thus the biological referential framework includes classes of plants,
insects, humans, etc. If the framework is assumed intuitively, as is
usually the case, we shall refer to it simply as an 'ontological framework.' If the case is otherwise we shall refer to it as a 'regimented
framework.'

8. We now introduce the term 'normative concept' to stand
for determined normative referents. If the normative concepts fall
within descriptive ethics and jurisprudence, their framework is determined implicitly or explicitly by the given normative context.
If the normative concepts fall within a normative system of ethics

and philosophy of law, the determination of their framework is made implicitly or explicitly by the author of the system.

If the philosophical analysis of normative discourse be considered but a preliminary, as indeed it must, to a philosophical study in depth of normative systems, then such an analysis will consist in (1) the investigation of normative concepts, if it is empirically oriented, of an existing normative system; and (2) if it is speculatively oriented, of a proposed normative system.

THEORY OF LAW AND MORALS
SUBJECTS AND OBJECTS OF SOCIAL CONTROL

I. *Individual*

1. The basic elements over whom and by whom social control can be exercised are individuals, in isolation or in groups. And since only individuals or groups of individuals can have rights, duties, privileges, own property or pursue ideals, all of law and morals represent in essence nothing else but the stipulation of permissible or impermissible, praiseworthy or blameworthy relations between individuals and groups of individuals, counting also the individual himself as capable of sharing such relations toward himself. Generalizing further, permissible or impermissible, praiseworthy or blameworthy relations can all be termed normative relations whose domains and counterdomains consist of individuals. Elements of normative-relations domains are usually termed in jurisprudence 'subjects' and elements of the corresponding counterdomains 'objects' of law.

Clearly, it is of paramount importance for the theory of law and morals to obtain a proper understanding of the concept of individual, as well as the concepts that are related to the concept of individual and are significant for the normative context.

2. The dictionary definition of the noun 'individual' is: 1a. a particular being or thing as distinguished from a class, species, or collection: as (1) a single human being as contrasted with a social group or institution. (2) a single organism as distinguished from a group. (b) A particular person. 2. An indivisible entity. 3. The reference of a name or variable of the lowest logical type in a calculus.[1]

The sense of the word 'individual' is clear and the dictionary compilers fixed the rule of usage for the word. Possible references are also indicated by the dictionary entry, but in a confusing way. They can be reorganized as follows:

---

[1]Dictionary entries for this part are from *Webster's Seventh New Collegiate Dictionary* (G. and C. Merriam Company, 1965).

A. The general term 'individual' can apply correctly to the universal class of entities the subclasses of which are abstract and concrete entities.

B. It can also apply correctly to the subclass of concrete entities falling under the general term 'human being.'

Normative context determines in this case the reference for the term 'individual,' since only individual human beings can become subjects and objects of normative relations.[2] The referential framework of the term 'individual' is biological and it is in terms of biological properties that the class of human beings can further be specified. One of these properties has broader ramifications for law and morals: the duration of membership of an individual human being in the class of human beings, which extends from, let us say, his conception to his death. We shall use the term 'horizontal dimension of the individual' to refer to the individual as he is at the given moment, and the term 'historical dimension of the individual' to refer to the sequence of $n(2 < n < $ life cycle of the individual) moments in the life of the individual.

3. Realization of normative relations is dependent ultimately upon the behavior of individuals and hence the social control intended by law and morals amounts to the control of behavior in so far as such behavior is normatively relevant.

The singular term 'behavior' is customarily used in psychology and sociology, whose subject matter *behavior* is supposed to be, as well as in ethics and jurisprudence. Important though the term is for the social sciences, the fundamental semantic problems in connection with it have not yet been resolved. We shall attempt such a resolution here in so far as our analysis requires.

4. The dictionary definition of the noun 'behavior' is: (1) the manner of conducting oneself. (2) the way in which something behaves.

The dictionary entry seems at first glance rather simple and

---

[2]This assertion could be challenged, since most of the juristic literature includes "things" (thus *The Institutes of Justinian*, tr. J. B. Moyle [5th ed.; Oxford: Clarendon Press, 1955], 1.2.78) as objects of legal relations. Hans Kelsen (*General Theory of Law and State* [New York: Russell and Russell, 1961], pp. 75, 86, 95), on the other hand, considers "things" incapable of becoming objects of legal relations per se, but only as adjuncts to persons. We accept Kelsen's views on this point and extend them to include moral relations as well.

obvious. On a longer look, however, the picture becomes dimmed. What is the reference for the elusive descriptions 'manner of conducting oneself' and 'the way in which something behaves'? The words 'manner' and 'way' introduce the note of elusiveness and vagary instead of determining a straightforward concrete referent that the singular term 'behavior' seems to require. The dictionary explanations are thus obviously useless in this case and will have to be abandoned in the attempt to construe the meaning of the word 'behavior.' The tabulation of the components that will have to be correlated in order to solve the problem of meaning for the term 'behavior' is: (a) the linguistic expression 'behavior'; (b) the sense of the term 'behavior'; (c) the reference for the term 'behavior'; and (d) the rule of usage for the term 'behavior.'

There is no difficulty with the linguistic expression since it obeys the rules of concatenation for the formation of written English words. It may also be assumed that the fluent speaker "understands" the sense of the word and that the rule of usage can be established by analyzing cases of application of the word. The problem of meaning for the word 'behavior' reduces thus to the problem of reference.

Now since 'behavior' is a singular term it purports to refer to a unique and moreover a concrete entity. Furthermore, since the purported unique entity is concrete, it must, at least in principle, be accessible to observation. And since it is the behavior of individual human beings, it must be possible to locate it in terms of time somewhere between the individual's conception and death. But, what is observable between an individual's conception and death? Obviously a sequence of phenomena that may or may not concatenate in patterns which we shall call behavioral acts. The referent for the term 'behavior' may thus be a single act; e.g., "His behavior was utterly objectionable because he deceived that poor girl"; or, it may be a pattern of such behavioral acts; e.g., "The behavior of the baby was charming." The referent of the term 'behavior' is thus rather diffuse extending from one act to a multitude of them. Assuming as an empirical fact that an individual during his lifetime can perform a vast number of acts (say n) but not an infinite number of them, we can say that the referent for the singular term 'behavior' consists of m individual behavioral acts $(1 < m < n)$.

This determination of the concrete referent for the singular term 'behavior' would be all that is necessary if we were interested only in the biological aspects of behavior and hence would not have to go beyond the biological referential framework. But, for social sciences, ethics, and jurisprudence, this is not enough. For, in order to solve the problem of reference with respect to the term 'behavior' for the needs of these, we have to pursue the psychological connections of the phenomenon 'behavioral act.' And this leads us to two sets of questions: the subjective and objective factors of behavior, together with the problem of voluntary and involuntary behavior.

5. The objective aspects of behavioral acts of an individual a_1 are those that are in principle observable by distinct individuals $a_2, a_3 \ldots, a_n$ and indeed by the individual a_1 himself if mirrors, motion-picture cameras, and other suitable equipment are drawn into play. Objective aspects of behavioral acts must be, therefore, observable in principle by any individual and from the outside, as it were. But the individual a_1, while performing his behavioral acts, undergoes certain experiences inside himself, as it were, which nobody else can directly observe, and these experiences, moreover, he can recollect. Thus, let the individual a_1 be administered an electric shock. Outside observers can look at his facial expression and other components of his behavior while he is undergoing the electric shock. Let this also be recorded by the motion-picture camera. The internal feelings of the individual while undergoing this experience are not observable by outside observers and as far as they are concerned such feelings may or may not exist. They have no direct means of either confirming or refuting their existence. Yet the individual a_1 while undergoing such experience may purport to be quite certain of what he is experiencing internally and perhaps quite unaware how he looks to outsiders. He may be quite astounded if confronted with a motion picture and recorded voice of himself and thus forced to compare the objective aspects of his behavioral acts with his subjective experience of them.

Thus, whereas the existence or non-existence of the subjective aspects of behavioral acts of an individual cannot be ascertained through direct observation by outsiders, such existence or non-existence can be ascertained by this individual beyond peradventure of doubt by simple introspection. Moreover, every individual is capable of doing the same for himself.

6. In everyday life as well as in law and morals, it is assumed that every "normal" individual can to a certain necessary extent coordinate the subjective with the objective aspects of his behavior. Thus, we would allow him to imagine himself a great conductor, but would think him crazy if he climbed up on the podium during a concert and attempted to force himself upon the symphony orchestra as its conductor. And, in everyday life as well as in social sciences, allowance is made for cases and circumstances wherein the subjective and objective sides of behavior do not coincide.

Many of the fundamental problems of psychology and sociology, such as those of motivation, attitude, emotion, awareness, and consciousness, are directly dependent upon the elucidation and solution of the problem of coordination of the subjective with the objective aspects of behavior. Unfortunately, the sciences of psychology and sociology have not advanced far enough to offer a reliable guide in these matters. But neither everyday life nor law and morals can wait until psychology and sociology have matured enough to be able to offer such assistance.

Hence, what we do in everyday life is to correlate the objective side with the subjective side of our behavior and expect that under similar circumstances other individuals will do the same. "Sympathizing," "empathizing," "putting ourselves in the other fellow's shoes," is nothing else but an attempt to correlate the directly observable or expected behavioral acts of other individuals with their subjective side.

It is no wonder that with such procedures, grievous mistakes about the subjective side of other individuals' behavior are often made. Not every individual is necessarily sensitive to certain painful stimuli. Some may even enjoy them.

Now to have to live with the risk of making mistakes and to proceed with extreme caution in individual cases is one thing, but to try to found ethics, psychology, or sociology on such foundations, or to make glib generalizations about "character" is another matter. Therefore, ethical theories based on "definitions" or "analyses" or "principles" of pleasure, pain, or happiness are bound to rest on dubious foundations for this if for no other reason.

7. The intuitive knowledge of subjective factors of behavior determines not only what will be interpreted as the motivation of an individual to behave in a certain way, but even more so whether his behavior will be considered to have been voluntary or involuntary.

In so far as the objective role of behavior is concerned, behavioral acts can be neither voluntary nor involuntary, but can only occur or not occur; in other words, the issue of voluntary vs. involuntary behavior would not arise but at most the issue of predictable vs. unpredictable behavior. Thus, the problem of voluntary vs. involuntary behavior can arise only on the assumption of the existence of subjective factors in behavior, the individual's ability to judge whether he performs or does not perform his behavioral acts in accordance with his choice, moreover the individual's ability to decide whether he will or will not want to perform his behavioral acts in the future, and lastly upon the assumption that outside observers can judge on the basis of their own experience and the individual's external behavior whether his behavior is voluntary or involuntary. We may add that within this scheme of things predictable behavior may be judged to be voluntary or involuntary.[3]

We are now ready to make these matters precise in the following fashion:

Let M be the class of all the behavioral acts that an individual a may exhibit during his life cycle. Then there are also the subclasses K and K' of M such that they are determined by the properties of being voluntary or involuntary. And for every element x of M x $\epsilon M \equiv (x \epsilon K \cup K') \& - (X \epsilon K \cap K')$. The existence of the classes K and K' is based on the assumption of the properties of being voluntary or involuntary, which assumption is made in everyday life as well as law and morals and can be partially corroborated, but not completely.[4]

The assumption of the existence of voluntary and involuntary behavioral acts is a *conditio sine qua non* for law and morals. And whether a particular behavioral act is voluntary or involuntary is

---

[3]We leave out of consideration the larger metaphysical issue of determinism v. indeterminism, together with the free-will problem. These fall outside ethics, in our opinion, and may be considered as problems of philosophy of mind.

[4]A complete corroboration would involve the solution of the problem of determinism vs. indeterminism.

determined in law by the legal machinery; in morals by individual opinion such as "He couldn't help it" or "He did it on purpose." Moreover, such determinations are made only on the basis of intuition and everyday experience with occasional help from the related sciences of psychology and sociology.

8. We have seen that in the use of the term 'individual' there is hardly any need to go beyond the referential framework of biology. It was only when we had to deal with the voluntary and involuntary behavior of individuals that we had to go beyond the biological and into the psychological referential framework. The introduction of the term 'person' will force us to go beyond both the biological and the psychological and into the normative framework of reference.

The dictionary explication of the noun 'person' is: (1) (a) a human being. (b) a human being as distinguished from an animal or thing. (c) an inferior human being. (2) character, guise. (3) (a) one of the three modes of being in the godhead as understood by Trinitarians. (b) the unitary personality of Christ that unites the divine and human natures. (4) (a) *archaic* bodily appearance. (b) the body of a human being. (5) (a) the individual personality of a human being: self. (b) bodily presence: *appear in person.* (6) (a) a human being, body of persons, corporation, partnership, or other legal entity recognized by law as the subject of rights and duties. (7) reference of a segment of discourse to the speaker, to one spoken to, or to one spoken of as indicated by means of certain pronouns or in many languages by verb inflection.

The dictionary entries indicate seven possible senses associated with the linguistic expression 'person.' Of these, the entries under 1, 4, and 5 indicate that the biological and psychological aspects of reference are initially included in the determination of reference for the general term 'person.' The possibilities under the entries 2, 3, and 7 can be eliminated contextually since they do not enter the normative framework of reference for the term 'person.' The context indicates that the sense adduced under the entry 6 is the fundamental one for the term, and this sense as well as the rule of usage is clear intuitively, but the reference has further to be determined.

The reference of the general term 'person' is ultimately abstract, although initially it was a concrete individual. That this is so may be seen by considering that a dead testator is a person in law although he has ceased being a concrete individual; or that certain entities such as corporation and state are persons in law but are not concrete individuals. Moreover, every concrete individual need not necessarily be the subject of law and hence the person in law; as an example of concrete individuals who are not persons in law we adduce the case of slaves.[5] Thus, not every person in law need be a concrete individual nor every concrete individual need be a person in law. The reference of the term 'person' is, therefore, a class of normative constructs which may or may not be concrete individuals. And the properties which determine this class and the membership therein are stipulated explicitly or understood implicitly by the given normative system. The fundamental property in all the known legal systems has been the property of being capable to be the subject of law, with its counterpart in morals as an agent capable of moral or immoral action.

The reference for the term 'person' is, therefore, included in the normative framework of reference and is determinable ultimately only within this referential framework. Hence, the properties determining the biological and psychological referential framework can play at most an auxiliary role in determining the reference for the term 'person.' Moreover, whereas the term 'person' is indispensable in law and morals, it is quite dispensable in biology and psychology, which can get along by using just the terms 'individual' and 'human being.'

9. The term 'personality,' though used in law and morals, is not of fundamental significance for them as the term 'person' is. In fact, normative systems could get along without using it at all. We shall discuss it here because it is used in law and morals in contexts wherein the term 'individual' and 'person' might be used, and because of its use within normatively relevant contexts by psychology and sociology.

This is the dictionary explanation of the noun 'personality': (1) (a) the quality or state of being a person. (b) personal existence. (2) (a) the condition or fact of relating to a particular

---

[5]That the reference for 'person' must not be confused with the reference for 'individual' was clearly recognized by Kelsen (*General Theory of Law and State*, pp. 93 ff.), who came to this conclusion intuitively and through knowledge of the law rather than by means of a semantic theory.

person; specific: the condition of referring directly to or aimed disparagingly or hostilely at an individual. (b) an offensively personal remark. (3) (a) the complex of characteristics that distinguishes an individual or a nation or group. (b) the totality of an individual's behavioral and emotional tendencies. (c) the organization of the individual's distinguishing character traits, attitudes, or habits. (4) (a) distinction or excellence of personal and social traits. (b) a person having such quality. (c) a person of importance, prominence, renown, or notoriety.

The linguistic expression 'personality' obeys the English rules of concatenation and its senses as well as its rules of usage are clear. The unresolved problem that remains is that of reference.

Now when we scan the dictionary entry under 1, 2, and 3, it also becomes clear that the reference to be associated with these is the same as the reference for the term 'person.' Thus in these cases even though the given linguistic expressions are different, their reference is not.

The entry under 3 indicates the reference for the term 'personality' as it is usually understood in psychology and sociology. Moreover, the reference indicated by 3 falls almost exclusively into the psychological frame of reference. In addition, the reference indicated under 4 associates value judgments with the personality traits listed under 3 and imposes thus an esthetic or a normative framework of reference on the term, as the case may be.

It is obvious, therefore, that the introduction of the term 'personality,' in so far as reference is concerned, is gratuitous since the same job can be done by using the term 'person' instead of 'personality' with the sense under 1 and 2, and by using modifiers with the term 'person' with the senses under 3 and 4. That the term 'personality' appears so often in psychology and sociology and that it acquired an air of indispensability is nothing else but an indication of a desperate groping and a naive handling of the problem of reference in these sciences.

10. Neither law nor morals can disregard psychological factors in normative relations. Indeed, the assumption of certain psychological states sometimes determines whether the relation between individuals is or is not a normative one. But since psychological factors cannot be ignored in normative relations, the question at once arises, by what means are such psychological factors assessed? And the answer to such a question is that such assessments are established by means of common sense, which is to say by introspective insight in conjunction with uncontrolled observation. That such a situation is unsatisfactory needs no argument. That law and morals will have to stick to common sense until more reliable methods are developed also needs no argument. But although no reliable means are as yet available, the awareness of the problem forces us to consider carefully the issues involved. This awareness was thrust upon us by the deepening of our understanding of the semantic and psychological factors involved in the difficulties.

As we have seen previously, individual semantic issues can be resolved, though general solution is impossible. Unfortunately, psychological issues cannot be resolved even for individual cases.

Now since psychology can neither offer a general solution to this problem nor deal effectively with individual cases, we are forced to this position:

Accept the common-sense explanation of psychological issues pertaining to individual cases, backing up such explanations whenever possible by insights to be gleaned from psychology, and refuse to develop general theories that presuppose non-existent psychological solutions.

One of the consequences of the position will be the abandonment of ethical theories that are based on the assumption that a general solution for these psychological problems exists, or that the psychological problems themselves do not exist. We have here specifically in mind various types of eudaemonism, with the possible exception of otherworldly eudaemonism, and hedonism.

II. *Society*

1. The dictionary entry for the noun 'society,' which at best offers only a vague indication of what the reference for the term might be, is: (1) companionship or association with one's fellows: friendly or intimate intercourse: company. (2) A voluntary association of individuals for common ends; esp: an organized group working together or periodically meeting because of common interests, beliefs, or professions. (3) (a) an enduring and cooperating social group whose members have developed organized patterns of relationships through instruction with one another. (b) A com-

munity, nation, or broad grouping of people having common traditions, institutions, and collective activities and interests. (4) (a) A part of a community that is a unit distinguishable by particular aims or standards of living or conduct: a social circle or a group of social circles having a clearly marked identity (move in polite society, literary society). (b) A part that regards itself as the arbiter of fashion and manners. (5) (a) A unit assemblage of plants usually of a single species or habit within an association. (b) The progeny of a pair of insects when constituting a social unit (as a hive of bees); broadly: an interdependent system of organisms or biological units.[6]

The entry under 1 and 2 offers the vague intimation that the reference for the term is a small social group. Here the reference is obviously a collection of concrete individuals with primarily a horizontal dimension and only secondarily a historical dimension which does not extend beyond the life cycle of such individuals. Vagueness can be reduced by introducing the term 'social group' as the sense for this reference. But even so, the reference cannot be precisely and in general determined in this case but only for specific purposes and contexts.

Explications of the entry under 4 and 5 can be eliminated contextually since the references intimated by them are not relevant to normative discourse.

---

[6]We also adduce two definitions of the term 'society' from a current sociological manual in order to show how sociologists use the term. Their usage of the term represents in our opinion a prima facie case for the need of a semantic analysis of sociological concepts that we are proposing. (Arnold W. Green, Sociology: *An Analysis of Life in Modern Society*. [5th edn.; New York: McGraw-Hill Book Co., 1968], p. 38).

a. A society is the largest group to which any individual belongs. A society is made up of a population, organization, time, place, and interests. The population includes both sexes and all ages. Social life is organized, primarily as a division of labor, within a common territory and on a permanent basis in time. Many common interests are shared; and all interests, common and specialized, are inclusive enough to make social life self-sufficient among the members.

b. Society is a group, but most groups are not societies. A society is a group which includes all the other groups of an organized population that has a sense of belonging together. A small band or an isolated agricultural village may be a society. Throughout most of the modern world, however, "nation" is synonymous with "society." A modern national society includes the effective organization of its people, and it includes the sense of unity and belonging together. Within each national society, of course, can be found thousands of other groups. (*Ibid.*, p. 50).

The explication of the entry under 3 is the crucial one for normative discourse and the determination of the reference associated with it extremely complex.

First, a subclass of this divided reference, the living members of the given society, consists of concrete individuals. This subclass represents what may be roughly called the horizontal dimension of the society. The determination, however, as to which individuals are members of the given society and which are not is by no means easy, since societies in most cases mesh at certain junctures. Generally, such a determination is easier in tribal societies, whereas in complex contemporary societies it is virtually impossible to accomplish in a precise manner. Certain criteria, such as living on the same territory, can sometimes be invoked as an aid in their determinations, but not always. Hence, no general solutions of the problem of determination of reference can be offered in this case, but only contextual specifications and estimates for particular cases.

Next, when we extend our considerations to include individuals that have been members of the given society as far back as its history reaches and those that will be its members in the future, i.e., when the historical dimension of such a society is introduced, then it becomes impossible in practice to determine with any degree of accuracy the membership of the reference class even though it is finite. At best, and that only intuitively, a delineation of the contours and profile of such a reference can be made. A number of vague criteria can and have been used for the delineation of the contours and profile of various societies. These can be said to include psychological, structural (social classes), religious, ideological, political, and cultural criteria. None of these is precise, and hence none of them can be used for an exact determination of the reference for the general term 'society.' Difficulties of this sort and the failure to recognize the problem clearly constitute the main hurdles for the social sciences on the road to developing a reliable knowledge of human societies.

However, though a general determination of the reference for the term is impossible, it is possible to reduce the vagueness for specialized purposes by introducing modifiers such as 'national' and 'international' to point out which kind of society is meant, as well as to introduce contextual specifications and even stipulations.

The general conclusion concerning the reference for the term 'society' is that its reference must remain indeterminate in general, which in spite of its drawbacks can still be useful, since the determination of the contours and profile can be determined for specific purposes.

2. The property that can be used for partial determination of the reference profile for the term 'society,' and that is of great importance for the theory of law and morals, is 'collective behavior.'

We have seen that 'behavior' is a singular term whose referent may be an individual behavioral act or a sequence of such acts. Strictly speaking, there is not nor can there be 'collective behavior,'[7] if by 'collective behavior' is meant the behavior of the society as a whole; there can only be behavioral acts of individuals who are members of the given society, past, present, and future. And in this sense 'collective behavior' is simply the arithmetical sum of behavioral acts by individuals who make up the society. However, the class of behavioral acts by individuals of a given society can be distinguished into two subclasses: non-socially induced behavioral acts by individuals (e.g., in unorganized crime), and socially induced behavioral acts by individuals. A further distinction can be discerned within the latter subclass: the distinction between the subclass of non-directed or spontaneous behavioral acts by individuals such as lynching, and the directed or planned behavioral acts by individuals such as murder instigated by a criminal organization which represents the execution of a planned policy or decision. One further distinction can be discerned within all the three classes of collective behavioral acts: the subclass of behavioral acts that are

----

[7]However, sociologists take a different view in this respect, as the following sociologists' definition of 'collective behavior' shows:

Collective behavior designates non-institutionalized and relatively informal patterns of interaction in areas where established norms are not responsive to ambiguous stimuli, are marked with contradictions, or are being contested by persons seeking change. In other words, collective behavior entails a "crisis" or a break in regular routines that brings people into contact with others in situations where customary reserve is suspended because conventional guidelines and formal authority, for a time at least, are inadequate or insufficient to afford direction and supply channels for action. In this sense, collective behavior may be viewed as a significant search for new meanings which, under some conditions, mobilizes acts to restructure social relations (George A. Lundberg, Clarence C. Schrag, Otto N. Larren, William R. Catton, Jr., *Sociology* [4th edn.; New York: Harper and Row, 1968], pp. 489f.).

haphazard and subclass of those that exhibit patterns and historical contours. The distinctions between all these kinds of behavioral acts within the reference class of the term 'collective behavior' are important for the social sciences in general and for law and morals in particular.

3. We introduce now the term 'moral rule' and in conjunction with it the terms 'morals' and 'morality.' We assume also that the senses of these terms are intuitively, and hence for our purposes sufficiently, clear, and proceed to determine their reference by stipulation; since our intention concerning these terms is not to explicate their meaning, but to construct their reference for the purposes of our theory.

We stipulate then that the reference for the term 'moral rule' be the stimuli intended to induce or prevent specific behavioral acts by individuals or groups of individuals. And we further stipulate that every moral rule must satisfy these conditions:

(a) It must be expressible in principle by means of normative declarative and imperative sentences, and hence be subject to our rule for determining normative words.

(b) Every moral rule must be either original or derived from some other moral rule.

(c) If the moral rule is original, then its source must have been some society consisting of n members (n > or equal to 1). And it must be possible, at least in principle, to connect the original moral rule with its source, although this may be difficult or even impossible in practice.

(d) Every moral rule must be capable of specifying which subclass of voluntary behavioral acts it purports to govern.

(e) The breaking of a moral rule does not have as a consequence its invalidation.

(f) It must be possible to establish both from the objective and the subjective point of view not only the form and contents of a moral rule, but also the compliance or non-compliance with it.

(g) A moral rule may or may not result in a moral practice commensurate with it, but a moral practice always embodies within it a moral rule. The term 'morals,' with the indeterminate reference to moral rules or to moral practices, and the term 'morality,' with the indeterminate reference to systems of morals, indicate this embodiment of moral rules within moral practices.

4. The general terms 'goal' and 'ideal' are of cardinal importance for the explanation of some aspects of individual and collective behavior; and they are also of cardinal importance in explaining the role of moral and legal rules.

The dictionary explications of both terms are straightforward and simple. Thus the dictionary entry for the noun 'goal' reads: (1) The terminal point of a race. (2) The end toward which effort is directed; aid. (3) (a) An area or object toward which players in various games attempt to advance a ball or puck to score points. (b) The score resulting from such an act—And the dictionary entry for the noun 'ideal' reads: (1) A standard of perfection, beauty, or excellence. (2) One regarded as exemplifying an ideal and often taken as a model for imitation. (3) An ultimate object or aim of endeavor; goal.

The senses of both terms are intuitively clear and so are the rules of usage. But complications ensue as soon as the question of reference is raised. First, both terms can have abstract or concrete reference. Second, the reference for both of them may be the same. Moreover, when the modifiers 'individual' and 'social' are prefixed to both of them, as indeed they must be since they are always implicit if not explicit, additional complications ensue. We proceed, therefore, on the assumption that the modifiers are introduced.

If the modifier 'individual' is prefixed to the noun 'goal' or 'ideal' then only that individual himself and no external observer has direct access to ascertaining of the reference for either the goals or the ideals of that individual. Hence, whatever inferences are made on the basis of external observation of an individual's behavior about his goals and ideals must remain indirect, and so must also remain the inferences about his motives and attitudes, which can be partially explained in subjective terms by means of the notions of goals and ideals.

Since for our present purposes the construction of a viable reference is crucial, rather than the explication of such a reference in various contexts, we shall proceed by stipulation.

We stipulate, therefore, that the reference for an individual's goals be the objectives that he expects to realize with reasonable effort; and that the reference for an individual's ideals be the ultimate goals toward which he is striving without necessarily being able to realize them. And, since an individual's goals and ideals are inaccessible to direct external observation, in order to be able to draw inferences about them one will have to depend on the individual's communication about them in verbal or some other form and on the individual's behavioral acts, which can be correlated with his goals and ideals only by means of analogies. That an individual's goals and ideals do not necessarily correspond with his behavior, assuming that he is willing to report truthfully about them, is well known; that reasoning by analogy carries no logical certainty, or even probability, is also well known. That in everyday life we have occasionally to settle for such dubious conclusions is also well known. Fortunately, however, in law and morals, reliance on such conclusions is not necessary in many cases. And it is our conviction that in a well-formulated normative system dependence on such conclusions can be reduced to a small number of cases.

If the modifier 'social' is prefixed to the noun 'goal' or 'ideal,' the possibility of external observation opens up, as well as the possibility of intersubjective checkups, indeed the possibility of deliberate planning of goals, if not of ideals. In accordance with these possibilities the following cases for determining the reference for the terms 'goal' and 'ideal' arise: (a) if social goals are planned, their reference can be determined as exactly as the planners wish, and in such a case ascertained intersubjectively as well as by external observers; (b) if social goals are spontaneously formed and crystallized, as most of them are, then the determination of reference for these terms cannot be made in general but only in specific cases, by sociological investigation or by stipulation. However, it should be added that in such cases determination of reference by sociological investigation is encumbered with a considerable number of difficulties, partly because of the underdeveloped state of sociology, and partly because of the inherent difficulties of the problem of reference here itself.

5. The dictionary explication of the term 'institution' indicates only vaguely what the reference for the term is, assuming that its sense and its rule of usage are clear intuitively. Thus the dictionary entry describes the reference of the term 'institution' as follows: (1) an act of instituting: establishment. (2) Something that serves to instruct. (3) (a) A significant practice, relationship, or organization in a society or culture. (b) An established society or corporation esp. of a public character.[8] We shall now make this description of the reference for the term more precise by stipulation.

Let the reference for the general term 'institution,' with or without the modifier 'social,' be the classes of mechanisms, as for example marriage or blood vengeance, which may be developed spontaneously or deliberately, for the purpose of organizing certain vital functions within society. And we further postulate that it must be possible, at least in principle if not in practice, to indicate such classes of mechanisms within the given society. The vital functions which these mechanisms are expected to perform may be of a normative or non-normative character. But, since even the functions of a non-normative character depend ultimately upon those of a normative character, it may be said without exaggeration that social institutions are instruments by means of which social order is established as well as maintained.

It is clear, therefore, from what has been said and in the light of sociological knowledge, that there cannot be any general determination of reference for the term 'institution,' but only determinations of reference for particular societies and specific kinds of institutions to which the general term 'institution' correctly applies.

6. We introduce now the term 'moral order' and assume that its sense and the rule of usage will be clear once its reference is constructed by means of stipulation.

We let the reference for the term 'moral order' be the network consisting of the following components: a set of moral rules; a set of practices isomorphic with the set of moral rules; a machinery operating spontaneously or by planning for adjudicating whether a normative relation postulated by a moral rule has been realized or not; and a machinery that will be set in operation spontaneously or by planning to enforce compliance with the moral rule in case of default.

---

[8]The sociological definition of 'institution' is: "A comparatively enduring and formal configuration of prescriptions, beliefs, and practices that is regarded by the group as essential for the maintenance of its structure and basic values" (*Ibid.*, p.753).

The existence of moral order, although here assumed, can be partially corroborated empirically for any concrete society. Thus, once a certain moral rule has been established it is fairly easy to verify whether, and to what extent, it is complied with by the members of that society, and even by outsiders. And by repetition of such a procedure the same can be accomplished for the whole set of moral rules. Moreover, the ability to predict the behavior of the members of a society is based on the assumption of existence of the moral order for that society. Thus, for example, assuming the existence of the moral rule "You shall not steal," it is possible to ascertain whether and to what extent its members comply with it, as well as to entertain an expectation of behavior, or compliance or non-compliance, with the rule. It is important to point out in this connection, however, that an infringement of a moral rule does not invalidate either the rule or the moral order, yet that a significant percentage of violations of a moral rule, or a large number of moral rules, will have a bearing on our assessment whether the rule or the moral order is operational or not.

7. We introduce next the correlative term 'social order,' assuming again that its sense and usage are clear, and proceed to determine its reference by stipulation.

Let us stipulate that the reference for the term 'social order' be determined by an unspecified relation between social classes. These further items have then to be elaborated upon: (a) the problem of determining the membership of a social class; and (b) the problem of specifying the relation between social classes.

The problem of determining the membership of a social class depends on our ability to ascertain the properties which determine that social class. If such properties are stipulated by law this job is relatively easy, since in such a case the legal system itself stipulates the required properties. But, unfortunately, in most cases there are no legal stipulations concerning social classes. Hence, one will have to do without them, and it is here that the real difficulties have to be faced: (a) it is impossible to design a general method for singling out relevant properties; and (b) even if such a singling out is successful it is difficult to decide which of them will have precedence. One could, of course, single out, as is done in sociology, such indicators as landed property, income, educational attainment, "moral qualities," etc. All of these are, however, vague and can be of only a limited use within the given social context. But even if we are successful in this regard it is still impossible to determine by any objective methods which one of them should have precedence for determining the class: landed property, income, educational attainment, or perhaps none. Yet it is possible to use such indicators for specific societies, within limitations, to determine not only the relevant properties, but also their order of precedence.

Now the stratification of social classes into a social order must be backed up by some means, be it sheer physical force, or economic power, or some other means, or in most cases a combination of such means. But these in turn have to be backed up because their sheer organization and maintenance would be impossible without certain rules that authorize their organization and exercise. Thus ultimately every social order is backed up by moral order, and this in turn, if we can rely on historical evidence, by a system of religio-ideological beliefs and practices.

8. We now introduce pairs of terms which are oftentimes used glibly in the social sciences, though they should be used sparingly if they must be used at all. They are: 'growth' and 'decay,' 'development' and 'corruption,' 'progress' and 'decline,' with or without the prefixed modifiers 'moral' and 'social.'

When these terms are used within the biological framework, their reference can be determined by specifying physico-chemical and biological processes, which are observable and even measurable. But when they are used within the socio-psychological framework, their reference is usually assumed to be observable if not always measurable, but in fact it is neither. To appreciate the confusion that is introduced by the very use of such terms we shall enumerate the possible references that are intended by their application.

(a) the terms 'moral growth,' 'moral development,' 'moral corruption,' and 'moral decline' can be used to characterize the 'growth,' 'decline,' etc., of an individual with respect to his morality. In such a case the "character" or "state" of an individual is assessed by another individual in order to establish whether the assessed individual is morally "improving" or "deteriorating." That such an assessment is usually emotionally colored and highly subjective may be left aside. What is important for our consideration is the fact that the reference of these terms cannot be determined even within the rather generous limit of tolerance for vague reference. For what reference is intended by 'moral state' or 'moral character' that is supposed further to be specified by the terms 'moral growth,' etc.? That the assessed individual observes all of the moral rules, or some, or none that are believed in by the assessor? Intuitive empirical evidence, which can easily be supported by controlled observation, is that no individual observes all the moral rules all the time, that some of the moral rules he is likely to break more often and without much ado whereas some he may never break. To convince ourselves of this all we need is to contrast the case of lying in everyday life with that of murder. Moreover, the assessor assumes that the assessed individual accepts such moral rules, which need not necessarily be the case. True, the assessor may blame the assessed individual even for not accepting a moral rule. Moreover, it must also be added that the assessor seldom considers the whole life cycle of the individual or even a significant portion thereof.

It is clear, therefore, that the reference for the terms 'moral growth,' 'moral decline,' etc., is hopelessly muddled and confused, and since their use is actually unnecessary in the theory of law and morals, it ought to be dispensed with altogether.

(b) the situation is even more quixotic when such terms are applied in assessing the 'social growth' or 'social decline' or 'moral growth' or 'moral corruption' of a society. And it is usually individuals who undertake such assessments of society. What growth or development could one have in mind when one says that a society is growing or developing or morally growing or morally developing? What decline could one have in mind when one says that a society is declining or in a state of moral corruption? Is it that one intends to indicate that a society has more or fewer moral rules, or that all or some moral rules are not complied with or not always, or not to a degree? Does one intend to indicate by the terms 'social growth' or 'social decline' an augmentation or diminution in the membership of a society or perhaps of some mysterious social qualities?

The terms 'growth,' 'development,' etc., when applied to an individual, are already stretched, in so far as their possible reference is concerned, beyond reasonable length, and when they are applied to society the application can reasonably be made only metaphorically. In this case, even more than in the previous one, it is best to eliminate them altogether and replace them by referentially more viable and precise terms.

9. We take up now a problem that is practically non-existent in tribal societies, but looms large in differentiated societies, wherein also the legal order begins to be differentiated within the moral order. This is the problem of the moral conflict of individual and society which is made possible by a differentiation of individual from social morality.

Assuming that any society can consist of n (n > or equal to 1) individuals, and hence that an individual can represent a society all by himself, what can a moral conflict between an individual and society amount to? Obviously in such a case it would amount to a conflict between two moral orders: the moral order represented by the individual and the moral order by the society with which the individual is in conflict. And since it is a conflict between two moral orders it must be possible to establish the points of conflict between them.

Assuming that there is a complete moral harmony between an individual and his society at some unspecified point of time, which can be expressed more precisely by saying that there is a one to one correspondence between the moral rules that the individual and his society hold; assuming also that for every moral rule the individual complies with it, or in case of infrequent violation is subjected to a sanction by his society; then these possibilities open up at the point of differentiation between individual and social morality.

(a) the individual rejects some moral rules, but continues complying with them.

(b) the individual rejects all moral rules, but continues complying with them.

(c) the individual rejects some moral rules and discontinues complying with them, but the social sanction is visited upon him for non-compliance.

(d) the individual rejects all moral rules and continues complying with some of them, and the social sanction is visited upon him for non-compliance.

(e) the individual rejects all moral rules and the social sanction is visited upon him for non-compliance.

(f) the individual rejects some moral rules and discontinues complying with them, but the social sanction is not visited upon him for non-compliance.

(g) the individual rejects all moral rules and discontinues complying with some of them and the social sanction is not visited upon him for non-compliance.

(h) the individual rejects all moral rules and the social sanction is not visited upon him for non-compliance.

And since we assumed in our consideration that society consists of n (n > 1) members this enumeration is exhaustive .

Now taking into account what is called in social psychology social interaction, the one or the other of the parties in conflict may yield to the other or both may make concessions and reconcile their differences. We shall say in such a case that one or both moral orders have changed. The term 'change' pertaining to morals or society is important in social sciences, and in this respect, so far as we know, we have offered for the first time a precise definition of what is meant by the term 'change.' This consideration can be extended to societies in which both of the parties consist of a large number of individuals. Furthermore, we take it as an empirical fact that societies are constantly changing, though very slowly, with respect to their moral orders, since they participate in a constant process of differentiation. And it is this process of differentiation that accounts for social and moral dynamism.[9]

10. The sciences that deal with one or another aspect of society are economics, cultural anthropology, history, comparative religion, psychology, and sociology. And the relevant philosophical fields are moral philosophy, philosophy of law, and social philosophy. It is well known to those versed in these that in spite of a tremendous wealth of accumulated material it is impossible to offer well-attested knowledge of society. The reasons for this situation

---

[9]Henri Bergson (in *The Two Sources of Morality and Religion*) introduced the vague concepts of open and closed society in order to account for social and moral change as well as moral dynamism. The general idea is thus his, but the precise determination of these concepts is ours.

are partly methodological and partly due to the complexities of social problems. Yet in spite of these limitations we are in a position to make intuitive assessments pertaining to moral and social orders, and, moreover, even to clear them up occasionally by empirical methods and logical analysis. And by their very nature such assessments will be open to criticism. Nevertheless and in spite of this, continuous assessments with due regard to these difficulties are in order and will have to be made, if for no other reason than that social life cannot wait until philosophically and scientifically unimpeachable evidence and procedures are available.

III. *State*

1. The sense of the general term 'state' as well as the rule of usage present no difficulties. The relevant portion of the dictionary entry for the term adduces this description of its reference: a politically organized body of people usually occupying a definite territory; esp.: one that is sovereign; the political organization of such a body of people; the operations or concerns of the government of a country.

The voluminous and sometimes controversial literature on the concept of state represents nothing else but attempts to determine in general the reference of the term. The controversy involving the concept of state is primarily due, in our opinion, to overstressing either the sociological or the juristic or the sovereignty aspects of state and making it thus initially impossible to offer a general determination of the reference for the term that must include all the relevant aspects.[10]

The reason that state cannot simply be identified with society is that instances are known where state comprises a number of different societies together with semiautonomous social orders.[11] And instances are also known where a society is distributed among two or more states.[12]

---

[10]Thus, for example, John Austin considers 'the state' synonymous with 'the sovereign' (*The Province of Jurisprudence Determined* [New York: The Humanities Press, 1965], p. 226 [footnote]) and Kelsen overstresses the juristic aspects of state (*ibid.*, pp. 181 ff.).

[11]The Ottoman Empire is a paradigmatic example.

[12]The Serbian society during the Ottoman period, which was distributed among the Venetian Republic, the Austro-Hungarian and the Ottoman Empires, is a paradigmatic example.

The reason that the concept of state cannot be determined by juristic properties alone is that the state cannot be simply identified with its law. Here also instances are known where law precedes the establishment of the state, as well as instances where law survives the demise of the state.

Nor is 'the state' to be identified with 'the sovereign,' since the linguistic sign, the sense, the rule of usage, and the reference of the two terms are different.

Unsound though the sociological, the juristic, and the sovereignty conceptions of state are when taken individually, there is no doubt that the sociological, the juristic, and the sovereignty properties must enter the picture in the general determination of reference for the term 'state.'

Every state consists of the individuals that constitute its population. They represent in a sense the biological substratum of state. The population of the state represents a collection of individuals whose size is delineated by the state. And if no other factors enter into the picture, then politically organized society is identical with the state, and the political order established by the state is nothing else but a formalization of the social order. Unfortunately, the situation is seldom so simple, since the property of belonging to the state is by no means an essential property that determines society. How complex the situation actually is can best be observed in the phenomenon of birth and death of state.

Before a state is born, the territory on which it is to be born must contain some society or societies together with a social order by the agency of which the state is born as a juristic entity. And in the same way, when the state dies, provided there is no biological destruction of individuals living on its territory, some society or societies together with a social order or orders survives the death of the state as a juristic entity. Nor is the birth of a state a simple legal proclamation but a complex process which depends on a wide range of psychological, social, ideological, religious, and political factors.[13] The creation of a state is thus a political organization of a collection of individuals which may comprehend subcollections opposed to the political organization being imposed upon them by

---

[13]These factors, which Kelsen (*General Theory of State*) brushes aside as irrelevant, make his theory of state one-sided.

the state creating political order. Moreover, the imposition of the political order by the dominant social order is not, usually, a simple application of physical coercion, but a process in which this whole gamut of factors plays a role.

We may summarize these remarks by saying that the reference of the term 'state' exhibits definite physical aspects, which are the territory of the state and the individuals inhabiting it, as well as sociological aspects, which are societal subcollections of individuals, organized and held together by a number of bonds that are by no means of purely legal nature.

But no state can exist and be sustained without coercive machinery. And such a coercive machinery cannot be set up without a normative order. And the crystallization of such a normative order, together with the formalization of a part of it as the legal order of the state, must be independent or sovereign; otherwise it would be a part of another normative order. Thus the legal as well as the sovereignty aspects of state are of paramount importance, yet not to the exclusion of the sociological aspect of state.

We adduce now the general determination of the reference for the term 'state.' The reference of the term 'state' cuts across physical, biological, social, and normative frameworks; its components are a certain territory, population, a body of rules by means of which it is organized and operated, and the coercive machinery by means of which this whole complex is maintained. Finally, the reference of the term 'state' has both the horizontal and the historical dimension. But the reference that we have just determined has only a horizontal dimension, i.e., it is of the state as it might exist at any time. If we arbitrarily let the horizontal dimension of the state extend to a year, then the general reference for the term 'state' is its historical dimension which consists of n (n > 1) years.

2. Analogously to the term 'moral rule' we introduce now the term 'legal rule.' Again, the problem of meaning reduces to the problem of reference, which is difficult indeed, since in concrete law and morals no general clear-cut distinction can be drawn between legal and moral rules. The lesson becomes especially poignant in the case of customary and international law. Are the rules of customary and international law "legal rules" or "moral rules"?

Moreover, even in the case of municipal law it would be impossible to interpret its rules without some regard to the moral rules of the given community; or for that matter without regard to certain non-normative interests.[14] Also, in many cases legal and moral rules are identical.

All of these considerations indicate that if we are to have an adequate determination of the reference for the general term 'legal rule' we must make that determination in such a way as to be adequate for both theoretical and empirical purposes.[15]

3. We stipulate now that the reference for the term 'legal rule' be the stimuli intended to induce or prevent specific behavioral acts by individuals or groups of individuals. And we further stipulate that every legal rule must satisfy the following conditions:

(a) It must be expressible in principle by means of normative declarative or imperative sentences, and hence be subject to our rule for determining normative words.

(b) Every legal rule must be original or derived from some other rule. If the legal rule is original, then it must have been either newly formulated or in existence previously as a moral rule. If the original legal rule represents a new formulation, then its formulation must have been accomplished by a procedure authorized by the legal order. If the original legal rule represents a formalization of a previously existing moral rule, then this formalization must have been accomplished by a procedure authorized by the legal order. Lastly, if the legal rule is derived, then its derivation must have been made from some original rule in accordance with the procedure specified by the legal order.

(c) Every legal rule must be capable of specifying what subclass of voluntary behavioral acts it purports to govern.

(d) The breaking of a legal rule does not have as a consequence its invalidation.

(e) It must be possible to establish both from the objective and the subjective point of view not only the form and contents of a legal rule, but also the compliance or non-compliance with it.

(f) Every legal rule must contain in principle not only the

---

[14]We mention in passing that a whole field of jurisprudence, the so-called legal hermeneutics, is concerned with the problem of interpreting legal rules.

[15]It is in this respect that Kelsen's theory of law fails. And it fails because it attempts to separate legal and moral rules by a tour de force.

command for performing or not performing specific behavioral acts but also a sanction for non-compliance.

(g) Every legal rule must be subject in principle to recognition, adjudication, and enforcement by organs authorized by the legal order.

(h) Every legal rule must specify the subjects and objects between whom it establishes the legal relations; and the possible subjects and objects of a legal relation are individuals and corporations, including the state as a corporation.

Thus legal rules are distinguished from moral rules in that the legal rules must be introduced by specified procedures. Moreover, there must be a specified machinery for recognition, adjudication, and enforcement of legal rules. Moral rules lack at least one of these components, and, what is even more important in some respects, the property of *specification* is lacking in all respects pertaining to moral rules.

Finally, the question arises whether legal and moral rules appear as separate classes of rules or whether they are subclasses of a more comprehensive class of rules. We answer this question by introducing the term 'normative rule,' which shall stand for either moral or legal rules. The introduction of the term 'normative rule' will allow us to refer to legal or moral rules in an unspecified way. It will also allow us to accommodate the concept of a legal rule that has become a moral rule by the vanishing of the legal order. Moreover, the possible contradiction between a moral and a legal rule ceases to be a contradiction between "morals" and "law" and becomes a contradiction of n (n > or equal to 2) normative sentences of the system.

4. The determination of the reference for the term 'legal rule' enables us to determine the reference for the term 'law,' assuming that its sense and the rule of usage are clear. We stipulate, therefore, that the reference for the term 'law' be the class of n (n > or equal to 1) legal rules.

This explication of the term 'law' is sufficient for general theoretical purposes, but not for many specialized purposes, because of a long-established tradition that classifies law into customary and positive, municipal and international, public and private. In order to complete our determination of the reference for the term 'law' we must now turn to these classifications of law and explain them from our point of view.

5. The distinction between customary and positive law can be introduced from either the juristic or the sociological point of view.

(a) The distinction from the juristic point of view can be best adduced by this quotation:

> At its origin, a custom is a rule of conduct which the governed observe spontaneously, or not in pursuance of a law set by a political superior. The custom is transmuted into positive law, when it is adopted as such by the courts of justice, and when the juridical decisions fashioned upon it are enforced by the power of the state. But before it is adopted by the courts, and clothed with the legal sanction, it is merely a rule of positive morality: a rule generally observed by the citizens or subjects; but deriving the only force which it can be said to possess, from the general disapprobation falling on those who transgress it.[16]

And further:

> Considered as rules of positive morality, customary laws arise from the consent of the governed, and not from the position or establishment of political superiors. But, considered as moral rules turned into positive laws, customary laws are established by the state: established by the state directly, when the customs are promulgated in its statutes; established by the state circuitously, when the customs are adopted by its tribunals.[17]

(b) The sociological conception of customary law views it in terms of an evolution of inchoate customs and mores without necessarily excluding the machinery for adjudication and enforcement.

We shall adopt here the juristic conception of customary law since our concepts of moral rule, morals, and moral order (which include sanction, but sanction without recourse to specified organs to adjudicate and administer it) include the properties usually postulated by the sociological conception of law. The term 'customary law' will then mean to us positive morality embodying within it moral concepts of the given society or customs. This interpretation of customary law will enable us to accommodate cases

---

[16]Austin, *The Province*, p. 31.
[17]*Ibid.*, p. 32.

in which moral rules have not yet become legal rules by formalization, as well as cases where legal rules have ceased to function as legal rules. Our conception thus makes allowance for cases of progression from moral to legal rules as well as for cases of retrogression from legal to moral rules, which neither the Austinian nor the sociological conceptions do.

6. The distinction between municipal and international law hinges on the issue of whether international law is positive law at all or whether it is merely positive morality.

It is generally agreed that municipal law is a class of legal rules such that there is: (a) a machinery by means of which its rules are authorized; (b) there is a machinery by means of which to adjudicate whether a legal rule applies or not; (c) there is a machinery to carry out authorized sanction. It is also generally agreed that sophisticated municipal legal orders satisfy these requirements. And it is also generally agreed that international law, quite like customary law, fails in some respects to satisfy all three requirements. Hence, international law could be incorporated without much ado into customary law, and relegated to positive morality, as Austin indeed does.[18] But there is still one item that must be discussed, since one may admit that international law is akin to customary law, yet refuse to relegate it to positive morality, as Kelsen does.[19] The reasoning of Kelsen is as follows:

> International law is true law if the coercive acts of states, the forcible interference of a state in the sphere of interests of another state, are, in principle, permitted only as a reaction against a delict and accordingly the employment of force to any other end is forbidden; in other words, if the coercive act undertaken as a reaction against a delict can be interpreted as a reaction of the international legal community. International law is law in the same sense as national law, provided that it is, in principle, possible to interpret the employment of force directed by one state against another either as sanction or as delict.[20]

---

[18]*Ibid.*, pp. 127, 142, 187, 201, 214, 215.
[19]Hans Kelsen, *General Theory of Law and State*, pp. 363 f.; and also Hans Kelsen, *Principles of International Law* (2nd rev. edn., revised and edited by Robert W. Tucker; New York: Holt, Rinehart and Winston, 1967), pp. 16 f.
[20]*Principles*, pp. 16 f.

The issue of whether international law is law in the same sense as municipal law reduces thus to the question of whether there exists a centralized legal order by means of which legal rules can be effectively formulated, adjudicated, and administered and whether it is essential that these elements be present. If the property of effective formulation, adjudication, and administration of law is considered essential and crucial, then Austin's view will prevail. And if not, then Kelsen's view will prevail. We side with Austin on this issue and consider international law to be included in customary law and, hence, to be a species of positive morality, though we are not averse to the retention of the term 'international law,' provided the foregoing is kept in mind.

7. The distinction between public and private law is an old one. *The Institutes of Justinian* adduces it thus:

> The precepts of the law are these: to live honestly, to injure no one, and to give every man his due. The study of law consists of two branches, law public and law private. The former relates to the welfare of the Roman State; the latter to the advantage of the individual citizen. Of private law then we say that it is of threefold origin, being collected from the precepts of nature, from those of the law of nations, or from those of the civil law of Rome.

And in addition to the distinction between the public and private law a further distinction within public law is drawn between constitutional, administrative, and criminal law.

We said previously that any legal rule assigns a legal relation among the potential subjects and objects of law. Since the relation thus postulated is a relation between individuals, including corporations and states treated for legal purposes as individuals or legal persons, there can be no essential difference between the legal relations postulated by either private and constitutional or administrative and criminal law.

The distinction made between public and private law in traditional jurisprudence, if it is meant to be essential rather than a mere matter of organizational convenience, cannot be maintained from our viewpoint, since we do not consider procedural differences in some legal orders as crucial in adjudicating matters of public and private law. Nor do we consider as crucial the differences in sanction in some legal orders, in criminal law as punishment, in private law civil execution. The fundamental components of the legal process, which are the legal rule, its adjudication, and enforcement by public authority, are present in public as well as private law. Thus from our point of view the crucial factor is that public and private legal rules are formulated, adjudicated, and administered in essentially the same way by legally constituted authorities.[21]

In summary, whatever distinctions may be drawn between the private, constitutional, administrative, and criminal law within diverse legal systems, they are for purposes of classification and practical arrangement only, and represent no essential and philosophically significant distinctions.

8. We introduce now the terms 'growth of law,' 'creation of law,' 'administration of law,' and 'legal institution.'[22]

The term 'legal institution' applies to instrumentalities by means of which law is created, adjudicated, and administered. By mentioning the function of creating, adjudicating, and administering the law by a legal institution we do not intend to suggest that the same legal institution cannot perform all of these functions. The idea, current since Montesquieu,[23] that there must be a separation of legislative, judicial, and administrative powers in the legal process in order to ensure freedom as well as the fair operation of law is not tenable, either from the theoretical or the empirical point of view. It is not tenable from the theoretical point of view because there is no reason whatever why one and the same institution could not exercise all of the three powers without abusing any of them. And, in fact, Montesquieu's doctrine was primarily aimed against the single-person exercise of these powers, rather than institutional exercise of them. Thus, it could be argued only that if a single person were to formulate, adjudicate, and enforce the legal rule, then in such a case the legal process would be subject to abuse. Neither is it tenable from the empirical point of view because: (a) legislatures usually have the authority, at least indirectly, to supervise the

---

[21]This is generally recognized by Kelsen (*General Theory of Law and State*, pp. 50 ff., 201 ff.) although from a different point of view.

[22]We assume that the sense and the rule of usage are clear regarding these terms and proceed to deal with their reference as circumscribed in jurisprudence, since these are basically technical juristic terms.

[23]*The Spirit of the Laws by Baron de Montesquieu*, tr. Thomas Nugent (New York: Hafner Publishing Co., 1949), pp. 140 f.

adjudication and the administration of law; (b) the law courts create as well as administer the law; (c) and finally, administrative institutions create and adjudicate as well as administer the law.

Moreover, be this as it may, the reference for the term 'legal institution' is still an instrumentality that either creates or adjudicates or administers the law, and possibly does all three. And this instrumentality in turn is created by custom or political decision. But even if it is created by custom its creation has to be formalized by specific law creating or authorizing agencies which in turn are ultimately authorized by political decision.

9. Law is administered by legal institutions, and hence the reference for the terms 'administration of law' is the authorized operation of legal institutions. Yet, although the administration of law is of vital significance from the empirical point of view, the specific ways of administration of law are relative, i.e., the specific modes of administration of law are subject to historical, political, social, and economic circumstances; and there are no restrictions upon the modes and ways of administering law from the theoretical point of view either, so long as the condition of effective administration is satisfied.

10. The term 'creation of law' applies to a particular way or procedure by which a legal rule is formalized, after it has been formulated.

There are two concrete ways by means of which a legal rule is formulated: by custom and by legal institutions. If a legal rule is formulated by custom, then it has to be formalized by a legal institution through an authorized procedure. And if it is formulated by a legal institution, the procedure by means of which it is formalized has to be authorized by the legal order.

11. The possible references for the term 'growth of law' are: (a) numerical increase of legal rules; (b) numerical increase of legal institutions; (c) improvement in effectiveness of legal institutions. But none of these seems to be intended by the casual users of the term 'growth of law.' Similar reasoning can be applied to the correlative terms 'decay of law,' 'disintegration of law,' and 'collapse of law.'

The use of the term 'growth of law,' together with the terms correlative to it, is not necessary in either jurisprudence or philosophy of law, and since it is ambiguous beyond repair it is best to avoid using it altogether.

12. Analogously to term 'moral order' we introduce now the term 'legal order' to apply to the network consisting of these components: (a) a set of legal rules; (b) a machinery designed to serve for the formulation and formalization of legal rules; (c) a machinery designed to serve for interpretation and adjudication of legal rules; (d) and lastly a machinery designed to enforce the adjudicated legal rules.

Again, the existence of legal order, which is here assumed, can be partially corroborated for any concrete state. And, once a certain legal rule has been formalized it is fairly easy to verify whether, and to what extent, it is complied with by the members of that state, and by repetition of such a procedure the same can be accomplished for the whole set of legal rules. Likewise, the ability to predict the compliance with the legal rules by those subject to the respective legal order is based on the assumption of existence of the given legal order. Furthermore, the violation of a legal rule invalidates neither the legal rule nor the legal order, although a significant percentage of violations of the same legal rule or of a large number of legal rules will have a bearing on our assessment whether the rule itself or the legal order is effective or not.

13. We introduce now the term 'normative order' to stand for the moral or the legal order, and consider the legal order to be the formalized and the moral order the unformalized part of the normative order.

The concept of normative order is crucial in relating morals to law, and largely because of to the lack of this concept, Kelsen, in our opinion the greatest jurist of the twentieth century, undertook the doomed-to-failure attempt to "separate" law from morals by means of his pure theory of law.[24] While it is obvious that for practical reasons some sort of "separation" has to be effected, it is also obvious that it is impossible to separate law from morals, if by "separation" is meant the establishment of two independent and unrelated orders. The reasoning that leads us to this position will become evident if we remember that it is impossible to formulate

---

[24]The most spirited presentation of this attempt appears in his programmatic *Reine Rechtslehre* (Leipzig: Franz Deuticke, 1934).

and interpret or even administer law without moral considerations. The moral order in all of these cases literally makes the background music of the legal order. In a sense, the controversy between the natural law doctrine and the Pure Theory of Law is nothing else but an overstressing of one side of the issue at the expense of the other side, and vice versa.[25]

Yet the resolution of the controversy cannot be found in stronger arguments for or against the Natural Law Doctrine, but in squaring the consequences of one or the other position and realizing that both of them are in conflict with either the empirical or the theoretical factors of law. The answer, in our opinion, is our concept of normative order comprehending the moral and the legal order.

But the resolution of the controversy between the Natural Law Doctrine and the Pure Theory of Law is not the only, indeed not even the main, purpose of our concept of normative order. The main purpose is the deparochialization of jurisprudence, as well as of ethics and the philosophy of law. These have been developed in the West according to Western patterns and are unable to serve the general theory of law and morals, which must be able to accommodate non-Western normative systems as well.

14. It is a historical fact that no human society has existed without some sort of normative order. It is also a historical fact that the so-called civilized societies exhibit within their normative orders greater formalization than the so-called non-civilized societies. But a greater formalization may result in the identification of law and morals at the one extreme or in a complete differentiation of law from morals at the other extreme.

Formalization of a portion of normative order, which means conscious planning, has to take place in complex social situations involving sophisticated economic, political and socio-cultural structures. Hence, we venture to predict, as the present economic, political, and socio-cultural structures become more and more sophisticated there will be ever higher degrees of formalization of norma-

---

[25]A clear presentation of the controversy from the Pure Theory of Law viewpoint is to be found in Hans Kelsen, "Natural Law Doctrine and Legal Positivism" (Appendix to *General Theory of Law and State*, pp. 389–446). A. P. d'Entrèves's *Natural Law* (London: Hutchinson University Library, 1951) offers a clear presentation of the Natural Law Doctrine viewpoint.

tive orders and less and less reliance on non-formalized moral orders within those normative orders. Thus reliance on law by future mankind will be increasingly greater, and the reliance on morals less and less. The reason for this is obvious: the obtaining of normative goals is much more effective by law than by morals. We venture, however, to predict further that morals will not vanish completely, if for no other reason than that it is empirically impossible to regulate all of human behavior by law.

15. We come now to the traditional problem in Western ethics and philosophy of law: the problem of morals vs. law and moral principles of individuals vs. the laws of the state. As the extreme case in one direction we may take states in which no differentiation of law and morals, at least theoretically, is allowed. A historical example of this case is the Sharia, and some contemporary examples are the normative orders in communist countries. In this case the problem of morals vs. law does not exist. As an extreme case in another direction we may take a hypothetical case in which a complete differentiation of law and morals has taken place, and, moreover every legal rule has as its counterpart a moral rule with which it is in conflict. We know of no historical example even approaching this case, and moreover think it empirically impossible, since it would entail that all human behavior be subject to either legal or moral controls, but not to both. However, as an empirically possible case we may take the example of a normative order in which some moral rules adhered to by individuals subject to the normative order are in conflict with the legal rules within the same normative order. As a result of such a conflict these cases ensue:

(a) An individual or group of individuals professing adherence to a moral rule in conflict with a legal rule comply with the legal rule but not with the moral rule. Or

(b) They comply with the moral rule but refuse to comply with the legal rule.

The resolution of such a conflict can then proceed as follows:

In case (a) the organs of the legal order may find the compliance satisfactory and leave it at that; or they may decide that it is prudent because of substantial opposition or the significance of the moral issues involved to change the legal rules in order to conform with the moral rules.

In case (b) the organs of the legal order may enforce compliance, which in the extreme situation will involve the destruction of individuals refusing compliance with the legal rule; or they may forgo the enforcement of the legal rules but not change them; or they may change the legal rules on prudential or moral grounds. But it is a standard practice in jurisprudence to postulate the primacy of law over morals in case of conflict. Yet it is a matter of expedience as well as prudence, and perhaps also justice, not to insist on the primacy of law over morals in some circumstances.

16. The classic examples of conflict between law and morals were presented by societies permeated by Christian moral ideas. Some Christian moral ideas were incompatible with the prevalent legal rules and some of them were outright utopian and could not have been seriously considered as realizable in the day-to-day behavior of individuals and groups of individuals. The history of law and morals as well as of ethics and philosophy of law in the West represents in many respects a gigantic effort to compose these differences.

17. The empirical investigation of morals is sometimes called 'descriptive ethics' and empirical investigation of law 'jurisprudence.'[26] The theoretical investigation of moral principles is sometimes called 'prescriptive ethics,' sometimes 'normative ethics,' sometimes simply 'ethics,' and sometimes 'moral philosophy.' The theoretical investigation of legal principles is customarily called 'philosophy of law' or 'legal philosophy.'[27] The usage of these terms fluctuates, and we propose to stabilize the fluctuation for our purposes by stipulation: we shall designate empirical investigation of morals by the term 'descriptive ethics,' and the empirical investigation of law by the term 'jurisprudence'; we shall further designate theoretical investigation of moral principles by the term 'moral philosophy,' and the theoretical investigation of legal principles by the term 'philosophy of law' or 'legal philosophy'; and we shall designate any of them by the term 'ethics' with the modifier 'theoretical' to apply to either moral or legal philosophy. Thus the primary object of our investigation is theoretical ethics.

---

[26]Related to these are sociology of law and morals as well as political science.
[27]Related to these are political and social philosophy.

SYSTEMS OF SOCIAL CONTROL

I. *The Notion of Social Control*

1. The term 'social control' expresses a vague notion of the control by society over a class of unspecified objects. As used by social scientists the term is intended to restrict the class of objects subject to social control to behavioral acts, which acts are to be induced or prevented, as the case may be, by means of social control. But such a restriction of the class of objects to behavioral acts will not be satisfactory without qualifications, not even in the social sciences. Thus in economics the control is intended to be over both the behavioral acts of individuals and non-live objects. However, this debility can be removed if the non-live objects are taken to be the property of individuals or collections of individuals. In such case the control is exercised by individuals or collections of individuals by means of property.

Using this interpretation, the domain of possible exercise of social control becomes restricted to human beings, and the term 'social control' in conjunction with auxiliary terms such as '. . . exercises social control over _____' comes to express a relation of m (m > 1) individuals with n (n > 1) individuals. Or, in a way customary in jurisprudence, the subjects of law by means of legal relations exercise social control over the objects of law.

2. But even so there still remains a vagary so far as law and morals are concerned. Thus certain behavioral acts are considered to be voluntary and certain others involuntary. Is the control to be understood only in the sense that it is to be control over voluntary behavioral acts, as indeed seems to be indicated by the customary usage of the term? If this were the case, then, for example, the behavior of enlisted men in time of war, which cannot be considered voluntary in many respects, could not be thought of as intended to be controlled by the enemy. But this is precisely what the warring sides intend, involuntary though they may consider the behavior of enemy soldiers to be. Hence, the intended objects of social control must be, in addition to voluntary behavioral acts, at least certain subclasses of involuntary behavioral acts. Nor can one ignore the fact that imbeciles, or even the physical environ-

ment, are intended, subject to technical limitations, to be the objects of social control. Yet here also we can reduce the problem of controlling physical environment to the problem of controlling human beings who in turn can control the physical enviroment. But we cannot reduce the problem of controlling involuntary behavior to the problem of controlling voluntary behavior. Therefore, we must conclude that by the term 'social control' the control of both voluntary and involuntary behavior is intended.

II. *Instruments of Social Control*

1. If the behavior of human beings is to be socially controlled, then it will have to be controlled either directly or indirectly, and furthermore, in most social situations, by means of a number of instruments, which we shall call 'systems of social control.' Such systems of social control in sophisticated societies are the normative, religio-ideological, educational-cultural-scientific, socio-political, and economic systems, and the system of organized force in the form of police and the military. We hasten to add, however, that these systems do not operate independently, but more often than not mesh their operations, and sometimes even move in opposite directions.

The systems of social control usually operate in institutionalized forms, but not always so. Thus organized force may be used as an instrument of coercion by means of institutional or non-institutional channels. For instance, legal application of coercion by the police would be the institutionalized form of coercion, whereas blackmail or even aggressive war, if the Covenant of the League of Nations and the United Nations Charter are considered as binding, would be non-institutionalized forms of coercion.

2. Systems of social control are either primary or secondary. A system of social control is primary if and only if by it all other systems of social control are authorized, but it in turns is authorized by no other system of social control. Thus the exercise of social control by economic means over individuals employed by a company, so long as the company violates no law, in other words so long as the company's control over individuals is authorized by law, is an example of the company acting in the role of the secondary instrument of social control. It is also obvious from this

example that it would be impossible for the company to act as the
secondary instrument without being backed up by the primary
instrument of social control, in this case the legal order protects and
authorizes not only the application of the economic power of the
company, but the economic power itself. Hence, in light of this
fact, it is obvious that the doctrine of laissez-faire in economics is
absurd. There is no laissez-faire in economics just as there is no
laissez-faire in any other area of social activities, but only more
centralized or less centralized, more circumscribed or less circumscribed, more delegated or less delegated exercise of social control.
Therefore, secondary systems of social control do not operate independently, but only by authorization of the primary instruments
of social control. So, ideally, there is always ultimately an entity
that can assign praise or blame for action or inaction within the
given socio-political order, and that entity is the normative system
as the primary instrument of social control.

3. The question can now be raised as to who or what authorizes the primary instruments of social control. This must not be
confused with the genetic question as to the origin of normative
systems. The answer, from the purely theoretical viewpoint, is: the
procedures that set up normative systems, whatever they may be.
Historically speaking, most of these procedures were religious in
nature, though in some cases they were political. But whether such
procedures be religious or political or both, they are always social
in nature. Hence, we may conclude that the ultimate authority
from which normative systems draw their authorization is society.
Societies may recognize, as indeed in many cases they have, as the
ultimate source of authority for their normative systems the grace
of God, the will of God, or any other entity of that nature. But
even in these cases the intermediate authority is society, where we
may stop, as it were on the administrative level, without going
beyond empirically verifiable entities.

4. Religion has always played a major role in the instillation
of moral beliefs and sometimes even a revolutionary role in changing the accepted moral views. Thus, without exposing ourselves
to the danger of exaggeration, we may say that religious institutions
and movements have always been primarily responsible for the
dissemination of moral propaganda, using the term propaganda in

its proper rather than derogatory sense. The influence of religion on normative systems was therefore always great; but how great has not yet been established with any degree of exactitude.[1]

Now, whatever may be the magnitude of influence by religion on normative systems, and however measurable such influence may become in the future, the question may and must be raised as to how this secondary instrument of social control is related to the primary instrument of social control, and the answer cannot be given in general terms. The relationship between normative systems as primary instruments of social control and religious or ideological systems of social control is thus relative, depending on particular circumstances and conditions.

An objection might be raised that religion represents a primary rather than a secondary instrument of social control, that in many cases religious institutions have had a commanding position vis-à-vis legal institutions. We answer this objection by noting that in every case of organized religion there is a normative system by means of which it is organized and administered; and hence, if such an organized religion does have a commanding position vis-à-vis secular legal institutions, it is not religion per se but the normative system of it that treats secular legal institutions as delegated and subordinate systems.

5. The influence of education, culture, science, and technology in controlling human behavior has been assumed to be very great indeed, ever since Plato, but exactly how great or in which ways such influence can be exercised nobody has yet gauged.[2] It is not surprising that those demanding social change, which necessarily involves some change in psychological attitudes, are not satisfied with the efforts of educational and cultural institutions toward that end. Nor again is it surprising that those demanding status quo are not hesitant to attribute great influence to educational and cultural institutions in effecting change. Hence their concern about

---

[1] Beginnings, and only beginnings, in this direction were made by Max Weber (*Essays in Sociology of Law and Religion*), Emile Durkheim (*Elementary Forms of Religion Life; Suicide*), and Jovan Brkić (*Moral Concepts in Traditional Serbian Epic Poetry*).

[2] By "nobody has yet gauged" we mean in any empirically verifiable fashion, not in the sense that assertions to that effect are lacking. Of these there is a plentitude.

what shall be or shall not be taught, which amounts to the demand for censorship, and, if the conditions are right, must lead ultimately to heresy trials and persecutions for heresy. Such a disparate assessment of the direct influence of education, culture, science, and technology upon society would not be possible if the belief in the great role of education, culture, science, and technology in controlling behavior were any settled matter.

Yet though we have no means to gauge the influence of education, culture, science, and technology in directly controlling human behavior, we do have sufficient evidence to indicate that their indirect influence on human behavior must indeed be great.

We have expressed doubts about the direct influence of education, culture, science, and technology on the so-called shaping of minds on the one hand, and asserted their great indirect influence in social control on the other hand. There is no need to substantiate our doubts. The burden of proof is on those that would maintain that we should entertain none. But we do have to substantiate our assertion that the indirect influence of education, culture, science, and technology upon society is great, which we do in this manner: In all cultures ranging from the so-called primitive to the highly sophisticated, a certain training or education is required in order to be able to perform most of the administrative, legal, and even economic functions. In the present state of civilization, and even more so in the future, it is impossible to perform most of the vital social functions without extensive educational, cultural, scientific and technological preparation. Present-day or future societies can be run only by a complex bureaucracy which in turn can be trained only in educational, cultural, scientific, and technological institutions. Therein lies their great indirect influence.

6. We group together miscellaneous social, political, and psychological systems of social control. Some of these are better understood than others, but none of them are understood satisfactorily even in terms of intuitive grasp, let alone in terms of verified knowledge. Nevertheless it is known that group influence on individual behavior must be, in some respects, immense.[3] And it is also known

---

[3]This has been established in a series of seminal experiments, the most remarkable of which are those of S. C. Chen and M. Sherif (cf. for further details Robert B. Zajonc, *Social Psychology: An Experimental Approach* [Belmont, California: Wadsworth Publishing Co., 1967], *passim*).

that no society exists on any sophisticated level without a tolerably efficient political system. Moreover, it is also known that there is an intimate relationship between political and normative systems such that neither could operate independently in any complex society.

All of these secondary systems of social control are extremely important, inasmuch as the primary systems of social control could not operate without the presence of at least some of them. In other words normative rules would be a dead letter without them. This can be corroborated by means of historical knowledge for the past, and we venture to predict that the same will hold in the future. But how, precisely, these systems operate, as well as how, exactly, they are related, will have to be left to future research in psychology, sociology, and political science.

7. Lastly, we shall take up economic systems of social control together with the systems of organized force, which comprise various forms of police and military organization.

Economic and organized-force systems of social control are intuitively the ones best understood of the secondary systems of social control. Thus it is well known that economic inducement can control a large number of activities by individuals and groups of individuals, as in employment, trade, and amusement. Economic means can even induce behavior that is in violation of normative rules, as in the case of prostitution, robbery, and occasionally murder. Still, however, it is not known with any exactitude how much economic pressure is sufficient to induce or prevent certain kinds of behavioral acts in certain individuals and under certain circumstances. Further development of these themes will also have to be left to future empirical research.

Now it is known by means of uncontrolled experience that application of force can induce or prevent occurrences of behavioral acts rather efficiently during short periods of time, provided that a sufficient application of force is possible. Yet it is also known by experience that the application of force is a crude method of social control, and in practice inapplicable over long stretches of time. The psychological and social impact of physical coercion over longer periods of time cannot be surmised even intuitively at present, let alone established in any dependable way. And hence these themes will also have to be left to future research in psychology and sociology.

8. The problems of the relationship between primary and secondary systems of social control and especially the problem of operation and management of such systems, together with the problem of centralization vs. decentralization of social controls, are some of the most intricate problems of descriptive ethics and related social sciences, both theoretical and applied. They are only of peripheral though fundamental importance to theoretical ethics: peripheral because their solution is to be sought in empirical research; fundamental because any normative system of rules will be in vain and fictitious if it is not or cannot be realized.

III. *Administration of Social Control*

1. Assuming that an individual can perform m behavioral acts during his life cycle, both voluntary and involuntary, and assuming also that they are all subject in principle to social control, we shall take it as an empirical fact that only a small subclass of such behavioral acts will be actually subject to social control. Assuming again a society that is to be controlled to consist of n individuals, then the total number of behavioral acts that could be in principle controlled in that society would be m $\cdot$ n. And again a very small subclass of the class of possible m $\cdot$ n behavioral acts would be subject to actual social control. Thus total social control over all behavioral acts of an individual or a group of individuals is possible only in principle. But, if we bear in mind empirical facts, we can speak only of partial social control, i.e., a total social control over an unspecified subclass of the class of all possible behavioral acts of an individual or group of individuals.

In either case what is significant here is that we can express numerically, and by finite numbers at that, the possibilities of social control in this respect.

Now let i (i $<$ m) be the number of behavioral acts of an individual which any system of social control intends to control; and let j (j $<$ i) be the number of behavioral acts that any system actually manages to control; and let p (p $>$ i) be the number of all the systems of social control by which an individual can be controlled. Then the number of the behavioral acts that the systems

intend to control is i.p and the number of all the behavioral acts
that they actually manage to control j.p. Then the number of the
behavioral acts intended to be controlled for all individuals in the
society is i.n.p; and the number of actually managed to be controlled j.n.p. Hence, the difference between the numbers i.p and
j.p, respectively i.n.p. and j.n.p, would express numerically how
strictly the controls over an individual or group of individuals are
applied.

The preceding numerical difference expresses one of the ways
which we have in mind when we speak of rigorous or lax law enforcement. But there is also another which we may have in mind
concerning rigorous, moderately rigorous, or lax normative code
enforcement. This pertains to the quality or degree of the application of sanctions in case of non-compliance. This kind of rigor vs.
laxness of the normative code cannot be expressed numerically.
So in order to avoid confusion we stipulate that the terms strict
and non-strict social control be used only when such properties
can be expressed numerically, and when the degree of social control
is to be expressed, that the terms rigorous vs. lax or non-rigorous
be used.

The situation, therefore, is very complex when all of these
factors are taken into consideration, and our analysis is poignant
indeed as soon as it is applied to certain terms customarily used
without much ado in social sciences.

Thus, for example, let us take the terms 'authoritarian society,'
'democratic society,' and 'permissive society.' All of them apply to
societies which are controlled strictly or non-strictly, or rigorously
or non-rigorously. But which of the p systems of social control
is applied in any of these respects or which of the respects are intended is not specified. Thus it is quite possible—and historical as
well as present examples abound to demonstrate it—that a society
may be at a given time strict or rigorous with regard to political
control, for example, and lax with regard to economic control. That
the former kind of society would usually be dubbed 'democratic'
and 'permissive' and the latter 'authoritarian' and 'non-permissive'
is a familiar fact to those acquainted with the vocabulary of the
social sciences. The implications of our analysis for the social sciences as well as for descriptive ethics are therefore obvious.

2. Both the primary and the secondary systems of social control can be analyzed theoretically in terms of policies as well as policy makers, and administration of policies as well as administrators of policies. But it must be stressed that this analysis will hold only in the ideal case, for in practice administration of policy is always to some extent a modification and even a distortion of policy because of inherent human and institutional factors, especially over long periods of time. A significant role is played here by the nature of the policy to be administered, as well as the circumstances under which it is to be administered. For, if the policy does not require bucking human inclinations and the institutional ranges of customary practices it should not presumably be very difficult or impossible to implement the policy, and vice versa. We say "presumably" because there is no established body of knowledge to aid us in reaching such a conclusion, but only accumulated experience.

3. An idealized model of a normative order would be analogous to a computer into which the policy has been programmed and the operation of the machinery, which in the case of social control would be the administration of the policy, determined by the programming. And analogously with the idealized normative order, assuming that the policy is within the range of the capability of the order, once a policy has been formulated, it should be realizable without modifications and distortions. But this is impossible in practice, as was indicated earlier, and hence the notion of the limits of social controls must be introduced in order to account for this fact. We have already the name for this idealized normative order, namely total intended social control with respect to the given systems. We shall now call the empirical factors that prevent the operation of the intended total social control with respect to the given systems the limits of social control.

The limits of social control can be minimized or maximized, as the case may be. They will be maximized if and only if the limits of social control come close to disappearing and the given order approaches the positive ideal. They will be minimized if and only if the limits increase to such an extent as to approach the negative ideal.

4. We touch briefly upon the problem of revolt and violence, which, although essentially problems of descriptive ethics and sociology, have bearing upon theoretical ethics. It is not known exactly what causes revolt and violence, but this intuitive guess will be ventured here: Revolt and violence appear to be the symptoms of the breakdown or serious impairment of the normative order on the policy or administration level. In cases where the policy is in question, certain normative rules are no longer acceptable to a substantial number of those intended to be controlled by them. In cases where the administration is in question the policy or some aspects of it may no longer be acceptable to a substantial number of those who are supposed to submit to it.

5. Correlative with the notions of revolt and violence is the notion of "respect for law and order." Again exactly what this notion is, and how one is to gauge whether or not there is or not respect for law and order, is a matter for psychology, sociology, and descriptive ethics, and only peripherally a concern for theoretical ethics. But it would not be amiss to guess that the more the limits of social control are minimized the more there will be respect for law and order and the more the limits of social control are maximized the less respect there will be for law and order. Lack of respect for law and order is then nothing else but a psychological attitude expressing the feeling that the given legal order has reached or is close to reaching the negative ideal of chaos either in terms of conflicts between the policy and administration or the policy and the moral sentiments of those to be controlled by the policy.

6. It is possible to draw blueprints for a multitude of normative systems. But not all of them need be realizable, given the limits of social control created by human, social, and institutional factors. Let us therefore call realistic those normative rules that are realizable, and fictional or unrealistic those that are not realizable. Then a system that consists of a significant number of realizable normative rules—and what that significant number may be will depend on circumstances—will be a realistic normative system; whereas a system that consists of a significant number of fictional rules will be a fictional normative system. We return thus to the basic point that no normative system can play a significant role in human affairs if it is unrealizable.

NORMATIVE AND NON-NORMATIVE CONCEPTS

I. *Tabulation of Key Terms*

1. A theoretical investigation of law and morals would be neither thorough nor complete if one did not take into account preceding inquiries into the subject. But this can be done by reviewing either the doctrines or the key concepts appearing in the relevant literature. Both approaches have been taken in the past and are being taken at present. The choice will depend on the purpose that one has in mind, and since our interest is in the concepts, the approach also will be conceptual.

2. The key terms expressing the respective key concepts that appear in the literature dealing with law and morals, including descriptive and theoretical ethics as well as jurisprudence and the philosophy of law, can be classified initially by our rule governing normative words into normative and non-normative terms. But whereas our rule clearly singles out normative terms, no rule exists that determines what are the key terms appearing in the relevant literature. A question, although not a substantive one from our point of view, can be raised about the method and the criteria for determining what the key concepts are. This question can be answered by saying that neither is there a definite method nor are there definite criteria for determining the key concepts, but there is a certain practice and consensus among experts as to which concepts are to be considered the key ones. This situation in descriptive and theoretical ethics as well as jurisprudence and the philosophy of law is nothing unusual. The same situation prevails in physical science, wherein the key concepts are determined by physicists in the same way, and likewise in other sciences: the determination of the key concepts is made by experts in a rather informal and intuitive fashion with presumably some sort of control by the demands of the subject matter itself. Yet these practices in scientific and scholarly fields are subject to a serious philosophical critique, which we shall advance later with regard to descriptive and theoretical ethics as well as jurisprudence and the philosophy of law.

Our procedure in the tabulation will be to single out the customary key terms appearing in the literature and simultaneously to classify them into normative and non-normative terms by means of our rule governing normative words. Moreover, we need not even tabulate every key term but only one of the cognates. Thus, the tabulation of the noun 'justice' will suffice and there will be no need to tabulate individually also the terms 'just,' 'to deal justly,' etc.

3. We tabulate alphabetically the key terms appearing in the literature of descriptive and theoretical ethics; they are also normative terms by our rule:

Adultery, blamable, charity, command, contract, deceit, disgrace, dishonor, equality, equity, eternal law, evil, fairness, faithfulness, fraud, freedom, guilt, honesty, immorality, imperative, infamy, iniquity, injustice, justice, justification, law of nature, lie, moral perfection, moral sense, murder, norm, obligation, offense, ought, pardon, penalty, perjury, person, praise, privilege, punishment, redress, repentance, responsibility, revenge, right, righteousness, sanction, sin, theft, value, vice, virtue, wrong.

4. We tabulate in the same way as above the non-normative key terms, that is, non-normative by our rule governing the determination of normative words:

Arrogance, autonomy of the will, beatitude, benevolence, blessedness, boastfulness, character, choice, common sense, compassion, conscience, courage, coward, cruelty, determinism, dignity, egoism, felicity, forgiveness, fortitude, free will, friendship, generosity, good will, grace, gratitude, happiness, hatred, heteronomy of the will, highest good, honor, honorable, humane, humility, interest of the community, love, might, modesty, motive, pain, piety, pity, pleasure, practical reason, pride, profligacy, public utility, pure will, purity, rational will, reason, respect, respectability, reverence, sanctification, self-control, self-interest, selfish, self-love, shame, sincerity, sympathy, temperance, ungrateful, utility, vanity, will, wisdom.

5. We next tabulate key terms appearing in legal literature and the philosophy of law which also are normative terms by our classification:

Abortion, acquittal, adjudication, appeal, arson, authority, authorize (to), bad faith, battery, breach of obligation, burglary, canons of conduct, charge, civil law, civil liability, civil litigation, civil right, claim, clemency, command, common law, commonsense justice, compact, compensation, complaint, constitutionality, contempt of court, contract, crime, criminal act, criminal intent, custom, customary rules, decency, deception, defamation, defendant, delict, delinquency, deprivation of rights, dishonesty, disinherit, disrepute, duty, equality of right, equitable, equity, essential justice, ethically or morally defensible, excusable in law, executor, exemption, fairness, faithful, falsehood, fault, felony, fidelity, forbid (to), forfeiture, forgery, forswear, fraud, freedom of speech or press, good faith, grace (of the Emperor), guardian, guilt, heir, homicide, honesty, human rights, illegality, immoral relations, immunity, impeachment, improper, indecent, indictment, infamy, inheritance, iniquity, injury to personality, injustice, institution, intentional misrepresentation, international law, interstate, invalidate laws, inviolate personality, irreproachable life, judge, judgment, judicial action, judicial decision, judicial declaration, judicial establishment, judicial legislation, judicial power, jurisdiction, juristic person, jury, justice, justification, larceny, law (of nature, positive, private, public), lawful, lawgiver, lawless violence, lawsuit, legacy, legality, legal code, legal duty, legal guilt, legal order, legal person, legal powers, legal redress, legal right, legal rule, legal value, liable, libel, license, litigation, malediction, malice aforethought, malicious motives, mandatory presumption, manslaughter, marriage, misdemeanor, mitigate (to), moral guilt, moral obligation, morality (positive), murder, murderous disposition, negligence, norm of conduct, obedience to the law, obligation, obligatory rule of conduct, offense, ordain (to), outrage, ownership, pardon, penalty, permit (to), person (natural), petition, plaintiff, plea, power (legal), principles of natural right, privilege, probate, prohibit (to), promise (legal), property, prosecution, public policy, punishment, punitive damages, rape, reckless conduct, redress, repeal (to), respondent, responsibility, revenge (to), revoke (to), right of privacy, rights (public), robbery, sanction, slander, social morality, standard of conduct, statute, swear allegiance (to), testament, testator, testimony, theft, tort, trespass, trial, tribunal, true faith and allegiance, unfair, unrighteous sentence, unscrupulous

journalism, unworthy conduct, upright and reasonable man, validity of law, value (moral), value of human life, vice, vicious and
dangerous propensities, vindication, vindicatory justice, violation
of duty, virtue, wrong, wrongdoer.

6. Lastly, we tabulate non-normative terms by our rule, which
appear as the key terms in legal literature and the philosophy of
law:

Benefit (public), character, common sense, conduct, dignity,
honor, humanity (in the sense of the Latin *humanitas*), humiliation,
injury (personal), intent, reputation, utility (public), voluntary,
wicked and cruel, will.

7. We have now finished the tabulation of the customary key
terms in the literature of ethics, jurisprudence, and the philosophy
of law. Our tabulation is the first one attempted, so far as we know,
and is fairly thorough in so far as the representative literature is
concerned. There may be here and there some terms that were not
included and that might be considered as key terms by some experts. This fact will not, however, invalidate our conclusions since
we are interested in the general and substantive issues and not in
the matter of detail and possible controversial peripheral cases. Thus,
at first glance at the tabulation one startling conclusion can immediately be drawn: the key terms in ethical literature are numerically
almost evenly divided between normative and non-normative ones,
whereas in legal literature the key terms are overwhelmingly normative with but a few non-normative ones. This conclusion will
not be invalidated by adding or subtracting a few terms either way.

Finally, we must add that all of the tabulated terms are pulled
out of the normative context, and hence in the interpretations of
such terms the normative context will have to be presupposed.

II. *Assessment of Non-normative Concepts in Ethical Literature*

1. The overwhelming majority of non-normative concepts
appearing in ethical literature are psychological. We have, however to qualify the terms 'psychological' and 'psychology.'

The term 'psychology' can apply to what was called psychology until the rise of experimental psychology in the nineteenth
century, or to a variety of it known under the appellation of depth
psychology, or to experimental psychology. In contradistinction to

experimental psychology, traditional psychology together with depth psychology may be called folk psychology; of a less sophisticated kind when practiced by common people, or of a more sophisticated kind when practiced by novelists, poets, philosophers, theologians, and depth analysts.

Our tabulation shows clearly that with the possible exception of the terms 'pain' and 'motive,' for which experimental psychology has use, all other psychological terms tabulated by us have been the preoccupation solely of folk psychology; and folk psychology has been notoriously unsuccessful in dealing with these most difficult terms of ordinary language with respect to the problem of reference.

2. Neither law nor morals can subsist without using the terms and the knowledge of folk psychology, whatever it may be worth, for experimental psychology leaves in the lurch those who are faced with making decisions involving psychological terms and knowledge. In fact, apart from a few seminal experiments and bits and pieces of knowledge, experimental psychology has not yet managed to be of much use in practical affairs.

But the heavy and uncritical use of folk-psychological terms by moralists, preachers, jurists, and other men of affairs as well as the common run of humanity is one thing; their heavy and uncritical use in theoretical ethics is another matter. And it is the uncritical use of folk-psychological terms in theoretical ethics that we propose to subject to a critical analysis and show for what it is worth. Moreover, we intend to show that the use of folk-psychological terms is in many cases unnecessary in theoretical ethics, and that in other cases they can be used in such a way as to make it possible to base theoretical ethics on sound foundations rather than the shifting sands of folk psychology.

3. It will be unnecessary to scrutinize all the folk-psychological terms tabulated in our list. A few paradigmatic terms which determine major concepts in theoretical ethics will suffice, since the same kind of analysis will apply to all the rest.

We single out for scrutiny the following folk-psychological terms:

Arrogance and humility, benevolence and selfishness, conscience, common sense and prudence, courage, happiness, pleasure and pain.

4. The dictionary definition for the noun 'arrogance' is: a feeling of superiority manifested in an overbearing manner or presumptuous claims. And for the noun 'humility': the quality or state of being humble.

The dictionary definitions of these two terms are by themselves telltale; for it is obvious from them that the terms are determinable only within a psychological framework, if at all. And what kind of normative rule, legal or moral, could one violate by being arrogant, or observe by being humble? Furthermore, always in law and usually in morals, an individual is neither praised nor blamed for having a certain feeling, or being in a certain state of mind, but only for committing or omitting forbidden or prescribed behavioral acts. Feelings and states of mind enter into the picture only for purposes of establishing the relationship between overt behavior and such feelings and states, in order to determine whether the behavior was voluntary or involuntary and hence excusable or inexcusable. There is, therefore, no sound reason whatsoever to consider arrogance a vice or humility a virtue, nor indeed to include these terms in theoretical ethics.

5. The dictionary definition of the noun 'benevolence' is: 1. disposition to do good. 2. (a) an act of kindness; (b) a generous gift. 3. a compulsory levy by certain English kings on the asserted claim of prerogative.—And the dictionary definition of the adjective 'selfish' is: 1. concerned excessively or exclusively with oneself: seeking or concentrating on one's own advantage, pleasure, or well-being without regard for others. 2. arising from concern with one's own welfare or advantage in disregard of others. . . . n. selfishness.

Parts 2 (a), 2 (b) and 3 of the dictionary definition of 'benevolence' can be eliminated contextually, since they are not relevant to the usage in ethical literature. Once that is done both 'benevolence' and 'selfish' appear as clear cut folk-psychological terms.

It would be difficult if not impossible to determine with any acceptable degree of exactitude whether somebody's disposition is "benevolent" or "selfish." It would be even harder to connect either term with a concrete normative system such that the observing of a certain normative rule would be the result of a benevolent disposition, or the violating of a certain normative rule the result of a selfish disposition. Nor can 'benevolence' in any meaningful way be considered a virtue, nor selfishness a vice. Therefore, since no realistic normative system can have any use for them, they are gratuitous in theoretical ethics.

6. The dictionary definition of the noun 'conscience' is: 1. (a) the sense or consciousness of the moral goodness or blameworthiness of one's own conduct, intentions, or character together with a feeling of obligation to do right or be good. (b) a faculty. power, or principle enjoining good acts. (c) the part of the superego in psychoanalysis that transmits commands and admonitions to the ego.

The dictionary definition for this term, as for most folk-psychological terms, is not very enlightening. The reason for this is that it is very difficult, if not impossible, to construct the reference for it. However, let us ignore the serious problems of psychological reference and stipulate that the reference for this term be: "the mechanism in an individual human being which adjudicates whether that individual human being has or has not violated a normative rule." Law and morals allow that such a mechanism may be impaired in an individual, or even if it is not impaired that it may mislead an individual on occasion. But they assume also, which is crucial, that such a private adjudication is subject to public evaluation and assessment, by means of informal public scrutiny, or by means of a formal public scrutiny in the law courts. Thus, although we must retain this term in theoretical ethics and philosophy of law, such a retention is at least subject to public scrutiny.

7. The dictionary definition of the term 'common sense' is: 1. sound prudent judgment. 2. the unreflective opinions of ordinary men.—The dictionary definition of the noun 'prudence' is: 1. the ability to govern and discipline oneself by the use of reason. 2. sagacity or shrewdness in the management of affairs: *Discretion*. 3. providence in the use of resources: *Economy*. 4. caution or circumspection as to danger or risk.

The senses of these terms are intuitively clear and the dictionary entries determine their references to a degree of accuracy sufficient for our purposes, since their use in law and morals, although essential, is merely auxiliary. For their use is hardly dispensable in assessing the accountability of individuals vis-à-vis normative rules. The concepts that they refer to are thus not elements of any normative systems, but rather the essential assumption or presupposition for operation of normative orders. It may also be added that prudence was thought to be a virtue, which is to say a normative concept, in traditional ethics. But this turns out, by our analysis, to have been a confusion of a norm with a presupposition for the realization of norms, that is for the operation of normative orders.

8. The dictionary definition of the noun 'courage' is: mental or moral strength to venture, persevere, and withstand danger, fear, or difficulty.

The sense of the term 'courage' is intuitively clear; and the concept referred to by the term represents one of the cardinal virtues of both the classic pagan and the Christian-influenced medieval and modern ethical theories. But by our rule the term 'courage' is not a normative one nor even an auxiliary one, for the property of being courageous is not essential in performing or assessing the performance of a normative rule. Thus the issue of courage does not arise at all in law and morals but only the issue of compliance versus non-compliance with the normative rules.

How preposterous is the subsumption of the concept of courage under the concept of virtue may best be illustrated by contrasting a courageous criminal with a cowardly law-abiding citizen. Even a pseudo-contradiction in terms might be divined here: on the one hand a criminal, the violator of normative rules, in possession of the "virtue of courage," and on the other hand a law-abiding citizen in possession of the "vice of cowardice." Our analysis debunks the pseudo-contradiction in terms by showing that there is no such thing as a "virtue of courage" nor a "vice of cowardice," that in fact neither courage nor cowardice has any business in ethics, but that both of them are rather dubious appellations and judgments of "character" or behavioral acts of non-normative nature.

9. Lastly we take up the folk-psychological terms 'happiness,' 'pleasure,' and 'pain.'

The majority of past and present ethical theories are eudaemonistic, which is to say that they are founded on the concept of happiness. And a subclass of these theories is hedonistic, since it interprets happiness as consisting in a favorable balance of pleasure, carnal or spiritual, over pain. Within our scheme of things none of these terms are normative, and the terms 'happiness' and 'pleassure' are in addition gratuitous to any ethical theory. Only the term 'pain' can serve an auxiliary function in ethical theory in so far as it is associated with the normative terms 'punishment' and 'unlawful injury.' Furthermore, 'happiness' and 'pleasure' are purely folk-psychological terms, whereas 'pain' can refer to either physiological or psychological varieties of pain. There is no need to go into the problem of reference for the terms 'happiness,' 'pleasure,' and 'pain,' since the first two have no significance for the theory of law and morals, and the third has only an auxiliary one. But, since it may seem rather arrogant to dismiss summarily what up to now have been considered the major concepts of ethics, we shall try to substantiate our position more extensively than the concepts of happiness, pleasure, and pain by themselves merit.

The crux of eudaemonistic ethics is *mutatis mutandis* the posing of the question, "What is the goal of life?", and its answer, which is "happiness." As the follow-up to this answer the usual approach is to attempt to determine the reference for the term 'happiness,' sometimes called the "contents of happiness."

Now the contents of happiness were believed alternatively to consist of worldly or other-worldly objects or states. Thus some thought that happiness consists in virtuous life, others in the pursuit of pleasure, and still others in the attainment of some object that would make men happy. The soteriological character of such a search in the case of religious or religiously colored ethics is obvious and needs no further expatiation; a soteriologically interpreted happiness can mean beatitude, which is to be obtained through salvation. But if beatitude is the goal of life, then the determination of the conditions for happiness is a matter for theology and not ethics. Observance of normative rules can be in such a case at most a condition for securing happiness, as is indeed the case in diverse moral theologies. In fact, moral theologies claim that the supreme dispenser of salvation may accord beatitude to the worst sinners, which is to say to the worst violators of normative rules, in preference to the best observers of such rules. Hence, whether the violation or observance of moral and legal rules is to count at all in the final dispensation of happiness will depend upon the supreme dispenser of happiness. Therefore, in the light of these soteriological doctrines, happiness has nothing to do with a realistic ethical theory.

The non-soteriological interpretation of happiness can be thought of as attainment of either physical or mental objects, or physical or mental states. But, if happiness consists in obtaining physical objects or states, then its purveyors could possibly be physicists, biologists, or economists, but in no case moral philosophers. Further, if happiness consists in obtaining certain mental objects or states, the issue of happiness reduces to a problem of psychology and psychiatry, but in no case to that of ethics.

Similar considerations can be adduced when happiness is thought to consist in the obtaining of pleasure and avoidance of pain, which can only be physiological or psychological states.

10. H. A. Prichard, in a well-known article, raised the question: "Does moral philosophy rest on a mistake?" We are in a position now to answer this question: In so far as it is a eudaemonistic sort of moral philosophy it indeed rests on a mistake, since it assumes either the role of soteriology or technology and economics, or psychology and psychiatry in disguise.

And, though it is true that moral philosophy has occasionally to deal with folk-psychological concepts, it is also true, as we have endeavored to show, that it does not have to lay its foundations on them.

11. Most of the non-normative key terms of ethics tabulated by us are those of folk psychology. The next greatest number are those of metaphysics and theology, and the remaining ones can be classified as being in the realm of economics, sociology, and politics. Of these we shall again select the paradigmatic ones for analysis.

12. As metaphysical and theological paradigms we choose 'determinism,' 'free will,' and the 'highest good' or 'supreme good' or the '*summum bonum*.' These paradigms in a sense represent a confusion in stages as the original intuitive concepts began evolving through sophisticated manipulation and hairsplitting, and the original layers were covered with metaphysical and theological layers, through the peculiar forcing of intuitive concepts of everyday life into ontological frameworks unsuitable for them. We shall indicate the stages of confusion first for the couple 'determinism' and 'free will' and then for the term the 'highest good.'

13. Let us say that an individual's actions are assumed to be non-determined if voluntary, and determined if involuntary. Further, the determination of an individual's actions can be induced by his physical environment, his biological endowment, his psychological endowment, and lastly the social environment.

It is clear that some actions of an individual are determined and some undetermined. In other words, some of an individual's actions are voluntary and some involuntary; moreover, some of an individual's actions will be borderline cases, difficult to classify as voluntary or involuntary. This situation is assumed in law and morals and can also be partially corroborated by internal observation, by which we mean observation within the human community. Should there be an external observing entity, say God, there is no guarantee whatsoever but that human actions might appear to him quite determined.

14. Now the solution of the problem of determinism vs. indeterminism with respect to physical environment would involve the solution of the problem of physical forces influencing an individual's actions, and then the solution of the problem of physical forces influencing these forces and so on until all the physical forces of the universe are included, if the universe is finite. And if the universe is infinite, then no solution of this problem is possible even in principle, since the naming of all the physical forces could never be completed.

Yet, though the solution of the problem is in principle possible if the universe is finite, its solution in the light of human capabilities seems an impossible task. Hence, a general solution of the problem of determinism vs. indeterminism with respect to physical environment is impossible.

However, partial solutions of individual cases are possible. Thus it is possible to assess in terms of common human experience whether an action of a particular individuals is or is not determined by physical environment. Juries, judges, and other individuals are doing just that when they assess whether an individual's action is voluntary or involuntary, that is determined or undetermined. And such assessing is always done on the assumption that some actions under certain circumstances can be physically determined and some not. Mistakes in factual assessment are possible and occasionally occur in such cases, but not legal or even moral mistakes, so long as the properly authorized officer of law or moral judges have made them with good intentions.

We can, therefore, eliminate from ethics the problem of determinism vs. indeterminism concerning physical environment, by relegating it to metaphysics where it properly belongs. So far as ethics is concerned the assumption that the vast majority of human beings are capable of making normatively significant choices from available alternatives is sufficient.

15. The problem of determination of an individual's actions that are due to biological endowment should be in principle soluble, and in fact many of the answers should soon be forthcoming from the rapidly developing science of molecular biology. But until such answers are available, the procedure of partial solutions for the disposition of cases before the law courts and moral judgment, as advanced with regard to determination by physical environment, will remain the only one in ethics.

16. The problem of determinism vs. indeterminism with respect to psychological endowment represents in its theological and metaphysical trappings the age-old problem of determinism vs. free will.

Let us assume for the moment that we can construct the reference for the term 'will' and let that reference be an individual's decision-making mechanism. Now, if such a mechanism is incapable of making decisions on its own, if it is, for example, like a computer that has to be programmed by an external agent, then its operations cannot be said to be free, since they ultimately depend on an external source. And if such operations are entirely independent from external sources, then there is such a thing as free will.

The common-sense solution to this problem, so far as morals and law are concerned, has been to assume that there is an independent decision-making mechanism within each individual, but that its decision-making processes can be influenced to a greater or lesser extent, depending on the individual circumstances, by external sources. Recent experimental evidence from social psychology tends to confirm this assumption.

Our conclusion, therefore, in this case also, will be as for the previous ones: no general solution to the problem is available, but only partial ones based on the assumption that there is an independent decision-making mechanism for each individual; and this will suffice for the purpose of ethics, since the deeper involvement with the problem belongs to psychology, sociology, and the philosophy of mind. Moreover, since the determination of an individual's actions by social environment reduces to the problem of external social influence upon his decision-making processes, this problem reduces also to the problem of how far external sources influence the decision-making processes of an individual.

17. The last metaphysical concept that remains to be tackled is the one referred to by the term 'highest good.' The composite term 'highest good' consists of the modifier 'highest' and the noun 'good.' The modifier 'highest' in conjunction with the noun 'good' entails that there are such entities as higher and lower goods. And indeed this is in fact an established doctrine of traditional ontology. In this doctrine the power of being is correlated with moral perfection, so that the lowest rungs in the scale of being are also the lowest rungs in the scale of perfection, and the highest rungs in the scale of being are also the highest rungs in the scale of perfection. But this whole ontology can be, and in our opinion ought to be, separated from theoretical ethics, which has no need for the lower, higher, or highest good.

18. A related problem is the one concerning 'good.' The term 'good' can be used alone, as an adjective, in which case it can be supplemented contextually by nouns and verbs, as for instance 'Peter is good' can become 'Peter is a good man,' or any other contextually suitable word, with 'good' thus becoming a modifier; or 'good' can be used as a modifier; or as a noun. As a modifier the adjective 'good' can be used in a number of ways, of which the relevant ones are those serving for normative assessments.

When 'good' is used as a modifier the normatively acceptable uses of it are those assessing behavior, as for instance "so-and-so performed a good deed" in the sense that so-and-so's deed conforms to a certain normative principle. But in such a case it is very easy to eliminate these uses from theoretical ethics altogether, rather than face the problem of constant vagueness and confusions.

The modifier 'good,' when employed in cases such as "he is a good man," can have this normatively significant use: "he behaves always in accordance with certain normative principles" or

"he habitually behaves in accordance with certain normative principles"; and analogously with "he is a bad man," or "he is an evil
man." But composite terms like these may best be eliminated from
theoretical ethics as likely to lead to the confusions inherent in the
dubious enterprises of folk psychology when involved in "character
judging."

19. We shall analyze finally the noun 'good.' It can be used
in a number of ways, for example 'the good and the beautiful,'
'man's good,' or 'the good of society.' In normatively significant
contexts 'good' occurs as a singular term, which is to say that it
purports to refer to a unique entity. But such a unique entity has
nothing to do with either normative rules or normative principles,
and only to a limited extent, notably in the case of 'the good of
society,' can it have relevance to law and morals, and in such cases
it can profitably be replaced by less muddy terms, for example 'the
interest of society.' Much of moral philosophy rests on the mistake
of introducing into it the pseudo-issues of "the good" and "happiness."

20. Our tabulation and analysis of the key concepts of ethical
literature shows that about half of them are non-normative, mostly
folk-psychological and after that metaphysical, theological, political, and economic. Our analysis shows further that none of these
are legitimate key concepts of ethics, that although ethics cannot
dispense altogether with the auxiliary use of folk-psychological
concepts, it need not rush into dubious generalizations and theories
based on them, but should isolate their usage as well as the use of
folk psychology to individual cases, and even then use them with
proper precautions and circumspection.

III. *Assessment of Non-normative Concepts in Legal Literature*

1. The key concepts in legal literature which are expressed
by non-normative terms, as determined by our rule, are not many.
In fact their number does not exceed five percent in our tabulation.
This is striking when compared with the incidence of non-normative terms expressing key concepts in ethical literature. Moreover,
even such a relatively low occurrence of non-normative terms which
express the key concepts in legal literature is still more telling when
it is observed that they occur as terms expressing auxiliary concepts.

How can this be explained? A plausible explanation, in our opinion, is that those who participated in the creation of legal literature were close to the facts of life, experience, and common sense, which served as checks against the wild generalizations and flights of fancy in which the creators of theoretical ethics indulged themselves.

2. The majority of key concepts expressed by non-normative terms which occur in legal literature are those of folk psychology. But the lawyer, the judge, and the jurist, when they resort to folk psychological concepts, are as a rule more cautious than the philosopher and the theologian. The folk-psychological concepts to which they resort are more circumscribed, more restricted by particular circumstances and context; they almost as a rule do not generalize.

3. We shall take as a paradigmatic example of a folk-psychological term often occurring in legal literature the noun 'intent.' Its dictionary definition reads: 1. (a) the act of intending: *purpose*. (b) the state of mind with which an act is done: *volition*. 2. an end or object proposed: *aim*. (3) (a) *meaning, significance*. (b) the connotation of a term.

The dictionary definition indicates clearly that the concept expressed by the term 'intent' is folk-psychological. And in legal literature the general term 'intent' is usually associated with the class of intentional acts. But which act is going to be considered intentional and which is not is left up to those authorized to make such a decision. No hypostatization of entities is in question here but simply a legal decision, not necessarily a factually correct one, as to whether a certain act belongs to the class of intentional acts or not. Such a decision is based on common sense and folk psychology and is hereditary only in so far as it makes a precedent. The concept of intent, however, is only auxiliary in the sense that it is instrumental in deciding upon the culpability in the violation of a normative rule.

4. As a socio-political and economic paradigm we choose a concept that is expressed by the terms 'public benefit,' 'public interest,' 'public welfare,' 'public good,' or sometimes 'public utility.'

The concept referred to by the terms 'public benefit' (and all the rest with the same reference) enters into law and morals at the stage of the formulation of normative rules, their adjudication, and their administration. And it is due primarily to this concept that the major confusions and pseudo-problems of deontological vs. teleological ethics arose. The situation is namely this: whenever a rational formulation of a normative rule, or its adjudication and administration, is to be made, the public interest must be taken into consideration. In other words, the creators, adjudicators, and administrators of normative rules, when acting rationally, have the public interest in mind in formulating, adjudicating, and administering normative rules. Hence they have to consider the consequences of their decisions. It is this aspect of the situation which has influenced adherents of teleological ethics to overstress it and overlook another aspect of the situation, equally important. Once a legal rule is formulated its creators expect obedience to it. Thus it is not left up to individuals to decide for themselves whether they want to obey normative rules or not. It is this aspect of the situation that was overstressed by deontologists, while the teleological aspect was overlooked. Hence, we may draw this general conclusion: both deontological and teleological theories of ethics are inadequate since they distort the issue *ab initio* by overplaying one aspect of the situation at the expense of the other.

IV. *Subsumption Methods of Normative Concepts*

1. The first attempt at a systematic subsumption of normative concepts was made by Aristotle in the *Nicomachean Ethics*. Many other attempts have since been made by moral and legal philosophers as well as by others, but none of them were successful, largely because of the confusions of normative with non-normative concepts.

The Aristotelian subsumption of normative concepts under the concepts of virtue and vice was incapacitated initially by the complex reference of the Greek *arete*, which consists of intellectual and moral excellence. The subsumption failed when it came to intellectual excellence since it proved incapable of being subjected to the test of the mean, as Aristotle himself recognized. But it failed in the case of justice also, since it too is incapable of being subjected to the test of the mean, as the painfully belabored essay on justice in the *Nicomachean Ethics* plainly evidences.

But the difficulties which Aristotle encountered in his subsumption attempts were by no means due only to the complex reference of the term *arete*. For if the intellectual excellence part of the reference be dropped, which is what Aristotle in fact did, "virtue" and "vice" could be used to indicate behavior in conformity or non-conformity respectively with the normative rules. It was rather Aristotle's involvement with folk psychology and soteriology that ultimately brought his ethical theory and those modeled on it into the morass of confusion and distortion.

2. The terms 'virtue' and 'vice' were never popular in jurisprudence and have not been much in use even in ethics since the nineteenth century. They have been supplanted for subsumption purposes by the concepts of value and disvalue, which are irreparably involved and confused, but have permeated the social sciences and general life through ideologies to such an extent that considerable attention must be paid to them.[1]

But in order to accomplish this task we must show first how the term 'value' is used in the social sciences, ethics, and the so-called theory of value, and then proceed with the dismantling job. We propose to accomplish this by a few paradigmatic quotations and a commentary on them.

3. A fair example of how the term 'value' is used in the social sciences is this: "It is, I think, implicit in morality that all human beings have the capacity for suffering and enjoying and for forming ideals, that is, of conceiving of ends having intrinsic worths or value."[2]

We may agree initially for the sake of argument that human beings have the capacity "of conceiving of ends having intrinsic worth or value." Let us also agree that it is somehow possible to specify in general what ends human beings may aspire for. In terms of folk psychology the ends would then be the objectives that men desire to obtain.

But what could be meant by the modifier 'intrinsic' concatenated with the noun 'end' or 'value'? Suppose that a man conceived as his end an income netting him $10,000 annually. What would be

---

[1]Cf. on this point William K. Frankena, "Value and Valuation," *The Encyclopedia of Philosophy*, VIII, 229–232.

[2]Morris Ginsberg, *Reason and Experience in Ethics* (London: Oxford University Press, 1957), p. 35.

'intrinsic,' or for that matter 'extrinsic' about this? The modifier 'intrinsic' is thus superfluous.

Now the end in our example is an annual income of $10,000. But the "worth" or "value" of this end is the same as the end. In other words the two terms have the same reference in this context. Yet the intended communication of the author is that ends have a certain property, to wit, "intrinsic worth or value." The vicious circle fallacy becomes quite obvious when we ask the question: Does the man desire the end because it has the property called "worth" or "value" or does it have worth or value because it is the end that the man desires? In either case if the man desires the end, he also desires the value, and if he desires the value he also desires the end. And we are left with the conclusion that the defining property of "end" is the value and the defining property of "value" is the end. Hence, the reference of the two terms is the same and the use of the ambiguous term 'value' superfluous.

4. In this quotation there is a hypostatization of 'value':
     But I do wish to point out at the very start that I am
assuming throughout that in some sense there are values.
Unless one accepted this, there would be nothing, in the
area here chosen for investigation, to be analyzed. Thus
the present essay is based on the assumption of the ob-
jectivity of values in one very broad yet not wholly trivial
sense.[3]

The hypostatization of an entity need in itself lead to no fictitious or non-sensical claims, and as an assumption it could be justified, provided that the hypostatizer can show either how to construct such an entity, if it is abstract, or how to confirm its existence, if it is concrete. But this is not what is proposed by the author of the quotation.

5. The following citations disclose in a nutshell not only the history of the term 'value,' but also to some extent and indirectly the reasons for the ensuing confusions:
     Values constitute a new theme in philosophy: the
branch of philosophy which studies them, axiology, took
its first steps in the second half of the 19th century.

    [3]Everett W. Hall, *What Is Value? An Essay in Philosophical Analysis* (New York: The Humanities Press, 1961), p. 1.

While interest in the study of beauty has not been lost altogether, beauty as such appears today as one of the manifestations of a peculiar manner of looking out upon the world, a manner called *value*. This discovery is one of the most important in recent philosophy, and consists basically in distinguishing *being* from *value*. The ancients, as well as the moderns, subsumed value under being without realizing it, and measured both with the same yardstick.[4]

The statement just adduced is in fact correct. What one has to wonder about, however, is why such a great theme of philosophy had to wait twenty-four hundred years to be discovered. And, moreover, what is so great in deciding to classify traditional ontology in a different way, to wit, by distinguishing being from value? Further:

We have thus far indicated three great sectors of reality: things, essences, and psychological states. At the outset, the attempt was made to reduce values to psychological conditions. Value is equivalent to that which pleases us, said some; it is identified with what is desired, added others; it is the object of our interest, insisted a third group.
. . . .
In overt opposition to this psychological interpretation of value, there arose a theory which soon acquired great meaning and prestige, and which terminated in the assertion, similar to that of Nicolai Hartmann, that values are essences, Platonic ideas.
. . . .
If, indeed, no one has tried to reduce values to the status of things, there is no doubt that the former have been confused with the material objects which enfold them, that is, with their depositories or carriers.[5]

Values are, therefore, neither things nor experiences, nor essences; they are values.
. . . .
We said that values do not exist for themselves, at least in this world; they need a carrier of value within which to reside. Therefore, they appear to us as mere qualities of

[4]Risieri Frondizi, *What Is Value?* (Lasalle: Open Court, 1963), p. 1.
[5]*Ibid.*, p. 4.

these value carriers; beauty *of* a picture, elegance *of* a garment, utility *of* a tool.[6]

Regardless of the designation, what is certain is that values are not things nor elements of things, but properties, qualities, *sui generis*, which certain objects called "goods" possess.[7]

Frondizi's presentation as well as criticisms are correct. There are indeed complex ontological schemes and presuppositions involved in connection with the term 'value.' He is also right in claiming that values are not things but properties of whatever objects may be in question. But he is wrong in claiming that only values are properties *sui generis*, for every property has to be *sui generis*, otherwise it would be identical with some other property. He is wrong also in assuming that we need "values" in order to be able to construct a theory of law and morals. For the concept of value, together with the theory of value, represents at best a dubious attempt at subsuming a very large portion of reality indeed under an all-embracing concept. Such a major attempt at subsumption would presuppose an ontology, or have to develop one, which is what in effect was done in the most grandiose attempt of this nature, Nicolai Hartmann's *Ethics*.

But we propose to leave ontology to metaphysicians and excise the terms 'value,' 'worth,' and 'disvalue,' together with their cognates, from ethical literature altogether, especially so since unambiguous and ontologically uncommitted terms are available to do the jobs which these terms are ostensibly believed to be capable of doing.

6. The method of subsumption of normative concepts under the concepts of right, duty, privilege, (legal) power, liability, disability, and immunity has a long tradition in jurisprudence and ethics. The method culminated in W. N. Hohfeld's *Fundamental Legal Conceptions as Applied in Judicial Reasoning*.[8]

Although Hohfeld's analysis and that of his predecessors was based on Roman and Anglo-American legal systems, its significance cannot be underestimated in view of the fact that most contem-

---

[6] *Ibid.*, p. 5.
[7] *Ibid.*, p. 7.
[8] (New Haven: Yale University Press, 1964). The original articles, of which this book consists, appeared in the *Yale Law Journal* in 1913 and 1917.

porary states are governed by means of either one or the other of these legal systems, and this includes International Law, if it be considered a legal system rather than a system of moral rules.

7. A standard method of subsumption in jurisprudence employs the concept of norm. The method in itself is correct and the term 'norm' determines the class of behavioral acts which are permissible or impermissible by the norm. Hence a legal norm expresses nothing else but what is expressed by our notion of legal rule. Thus the legal rule prohibiting stealing determines the class of forbidden behavioral acts in the same way as the norm prohibiting stealing.

In both cases the multiplicity of behavioral acts of stealing is subsumed under the legal rule or the legal norm. The only reason why we propose to use the term 'legal rule' instead of the term 'norm' is the logical precision and lack of misuse of the former when contrasted with the latter.

8. Instances of behavioral acts, past, present, and future, are subsumed under a normative rule, which in turn is an element in the system of normative rules. But a system of normative rules, as we have seen, may contain contradictions, or it may have more or fewer normative rules. Hence in this respect normative systems are similar to language; if they are not dead, then they are unfinished or open in the sense that the system may drop some normative rules or acquire others.

Now whether a behavioral act falls under the normative rule, that is, is an instance of it, is determined by the rule itself, well or poorly as the case may be. And in this sense every normative rule has a consequence, namely that some behavioral acts fall under it and some do not.

The fundamental question now arises: Are normative rules themselves consequences of other rules such that the former are implied by the latter? The answer to this question is in the negative. Although it is quite possible to create normative rules in such a way that some may be logically implied by others, there must be at least a certain number of normative rules that are ultimate in the sense that they are logically implied by no other normative rules, since the number of normative rules in an empirically feasible system is finite.

We now pursue the question further: Since there are some normative rules that are logically implied by no other normative rules, how do these normative rules come into existence? This is not a logical but an empirical question, and the answer is: Through the legislative process, in the case of legal rules, and through the social process, in the case of moral rules.

V. *Creation and Evaluation of Normative Rules*

1. The creation and evaluation of normative rules in a functioning normative system is a continuing process. The question that must now be raised is: What are the factors that are instrumental in this process? The number of factors would obviously have to be finite, if empirical limitations are borne in mind, and they must be borne in mind when dealing with a realistic normative system. But although the number of these factors is finite, it must remain unspecified, since empirical limitations make it impossible to enumerate all of them.

Yet, though it is impossible to enumerate all of them, it is possible to list them fairly exhaustively in these clusters: (a) moral and legal principles; (b) psychological and socio-economic factors; (c) religious and ideological convictions; (d) historical heritage and tradition; (e) considerations of effectiveness and realizability; (f) considerations of utility; and (g) considerations of rationality.

Not all of these factors are necessarily instrumental in the creation and evaluation of a given normative rule, but at least some of them are. And of primary interest to theoretical ethics are undoubtedly the factors listed under (a), (e), (f), and (g), which will be dealt with at length.

2. The fact that psychological, socio-economic, historical, and traditional factors play a significant role in the creation and evaluation of law and morals has been known since antiquity. And the Marxist legal and moral philosophy has justly drawn attention to the importance of socio-economic factors in the creation and evaluation of normative rules.

But the Marxist insistence that socio-economic factors play the primary or even the sole role in the creation and evaluation of normative rules is a distortion of the situation. Indeed, the issue not only of socio-economic but also of psychological and historical factors is best considered, so far as theoretical ethics is concerned, together with the factors of effectiveness, realizability, utility, and rationality. The reason that we mentioned them separately is the fear of being misunderstood as wishing to exclude them as of no consequence to law and morals.

3. Among the most serious errors of Kelsen's Pure Theory of Law is his conviction that religious and ideological factors can be eliminated from the scientific study of law. They can be neither isolated nor eliminated. The creation of normative rules, which in most cases involves simultaneously their evaluation; and the interpretation of normative rules, which necessitates further adjustments to the realities of life, and even distortions through adjudication and administration—these are made by human beings. And human beings cannot but be religiously or ideologically motivated, whatever that religion or ideology may be.

Past and present evidence is overwhelming in support of the opposite thesis, namely that religion or ideology have had and probably will continue to have an enormous influence, sometimes harmful, on law and morals. What scientific research can do is not to exorcise them by pronouncements, but to take them duly into consideration, as was done in classic anthropological, psychological and sociological studies of religio-ideological phenomena.

4. A subclass of normative concepts which we shall call moral and legal, or, jointly, normative principles have been scrutinized thoroughly in many normative systems, from many points of view, and will probably continue to be scrutinized in the future.

Not all of the normative principles need play a role in the creation and evaluation of the rules of a given normative system. But some may play a role in one and some others in another normative system, and some other normative principles, unknown at present, may appear that may play a role at some future time. Yet in spite of these theoretical possibilities, it is astonishing to realize that practically no known normative systems have been lacking a few fundamental normative principles, as for instance that of justice.

5. H. A. Prichard's question "Does Moral Philosophy Rest on a Mistake?" was answered by us affirmatively, by citing the confusion of normative with non-normative concepts as one of the reasons. Other reasons are the confusion of normative rules with nor-

mative principles, the confusion of consequences of normative rules
with normative principles, and lastly the explicit or implicit assumption that normative rules are logical consequences of normative
principles.

6. That normative principles cannot be used for subsumption
purposes should have been clear to moral and legal philosophers on
logical grounds. Normative principles are singular terms purporting
to refer to unique entities, not classes of entities. We show this by
adducing major normative principles and their opposites in Western
normative literature, and most of their equivalents can be found in
non-Western normative literature: (a) justice and injustice; (b)
legality and illegality; (c) equality and inequality; (d) equity and
inequity; (e) freedom and slavery.[9]

But only general terms can serve for purposes of subsumption.
Singular terms can subsume only the unique object to which they
refer, and in the case of normative principles the unique objects
are the purported abstract entities to which normative principles
refer. The logical issues here involved were vaguely known to
Plato, and the concept of participation was introduced by him in
order to enable him to deal with these issues. The problem of Plato
was that he thought, and justly so, that there is some sort of relationship between justice, for example, and just deeds, individuals,
and laws, but not a relationship of subsumption. For some time he
believed that the concept of participation determines this relationship, but later on in the *Parmenides* he expressed his doubts about
the adequacy of the concept of participation, and then he died
while attempting to solve the problem. To our knowledge nobody
after Plato has grasped the significance of this problem, let alone
tried to resolve it. Yet it is precisely at this point that theoretical
ethics becomes eminently relevant to practical issues in law and
morals as well as to other spheres of human existence, since they
all presuppose normative ordering of human relations.

7. The classes of problems involving normative principles can
be enumerated in this way: (a) logical problems which will have
to be tackled at the point where Plato left them; (b) non-logical
problems, which are the ones usually discussed in ethical and legal

---

[9]The only term among these that functions occasionally as a general term is
'freedom.'

literature; and (c) problems arising from application of normative principles in the creation and evaluation of normative rules.

8. The principle of justice is a crucial one for all known normative systems. We consider first the logical problems associated with it.

'Justice' and 'injustice' are singular terms. Their senses and rules of usage present no difficulties. But it is their problem of reference that engenders explicit and implicit controversies. But before attempting to tackle the problem of reference we must introduce the cognates, which play a great role in the discussions of justice and injustice.

The cognates are the adjectives 'just' and 'unjust,' and the adverbs 'justly' and 'unjustly.' Now, the cognates when used alone or in conjunction with other terms, are general terms. Thus, "This law is just" and "He was justly sentenced to imprisonment." But, since the terms formed in this way are general they can serve as subsumption concepts. In other words, "This law is just" can be subsumed under the concept of just objects or entities, and "He was justly sentenced to imprisonment" can be subsumed under the concept of individuals justly sentenced to imprisonment.

Now, semantic problems connected with general terms like these are by no means easy, but the relations between them and objects which they purport to determine are clear. And it is also clear for semantic and logical reasons that the problem of reference for the singular terms 'justice' and 'injustice' cannot be resolved by simply identifying their reference with the reference of their cognates. A major source of confusion in the history of these terms has been precisely the belief that such an identification of reference is possible.

Another common attempt to "define" 'justice' is by identifying its reference with the reference of 'righteousness' and 'fairness.'[10] But such an identification would not be very helpful, even if it were correct, since all it could accomplish would be to show that the referent for both terms is the same, not what it is.

But even if such an identification were correct there would

---

[10]A notable recent attempt in this tradition of explaining justice in terms of fairness is the one by John Rawls ("Justice as Fairness," *The Journal of Philosophy*, LIV [1957], 653–662.

still be left the problem of subsumption. For the only object that could be subsumed under the concept justice or fairness would be the unique object they purport to refer to.

The case would be similar if we were in a position to describe such a unique entity. For example, take the singular term 'Socrates.' Its referent could be described by specifying parts of it, for instance, the head, the heart, etc. But neither the head nor the heart nor any other part of Socrates could be said to be subsumed under the referent. And yet this is precisely what has been attempted with the concept of justice.

Our general conclusion with respect to the logic and semantics of 'justice,' 'injustice,' and their cognates is: only in the case of the cognates but not in the case of the concepts of 'justice' and 'injustice' can there be a subsumption and hence a logical relation between them.

9. We now raise the fundamental question: Since it is palpably false to attribute a logical relation of subsumption to the concepts of justice and injustice and the entities they are supposed to subsume; and since we run into the same problem when we try to determine the membership of the class of just or unjust entities, how is it that mankind proceeds on the assumption that we somehow "know" what justice and injustice are, and can assess whether an act or law is just or unjust? The answer to this question has been given, in our opinion, by phenomenologically oriented philosophy, namely, "by the emotional feeling for moral and legal principles." The notion "emotional feeling for moral and legal principles" is admittedly vague, but could be made more precise by further psychological investigation.

Moreover, justice and injustice are not logical opposites, but emotional opposites, just as love and hate are. Thus lack of justice is by no means injustice, nor is lack of love hate. Nor is lack of injustice justice, or lack of hate love. Nor is it true that we do not "know" what justice and injustice are.

Thus the emotional feeling for normative principles discloses to us the emotional reference for all of them, which is simple and cannot be further reduced to simpler components. Hence 'justice' and 'injustice' are singular terms which refer to concepts subject to no further logical analysis but to determination by the emotional feeling for them, just as for love and hate. Therefore it is not logic but the emotional feeling for justice that ultimately determines whether a law or an act is just or unjust.

The groping and grasping for concepts such as equality, fairness, righteousness, by means of which to explain justice in the history of ethics from Plato to John Rawls are nothing else but attempts to explain rationally the emotional construct which is the principle of justice.

10. The concepts of justice and injustice, though not subject to further logical analyses, need not be irrational nor subjective in the sense that the emotional feeling for them is peculiar to a particular individual only. There is of course a subjective aspect to them in that they are emotional referents subject to the individual's emotional feeling and experience. But there is also an objective aspect to them in that they are subject to the collective emotional feeling of large social groups and the largest of them all, mankind.

11. Lastly, we have to solve one more problem, which is the relativity of justice in particular and normative principles in general. Our answer is that there is a certain relativity in them because these principles are not finished products, but plastic constructs subject to development and refinement. Yet there is also a stability and permanence in them, as with any object that is in the process of development. This is nothing new, or peculiar to normative principles. The same situation prevails in all life. All law and morals are in the process of development and in a sense represent nothing else but the intuition of mankind at work, engaged in a constant process of creating, modifying, and sometimes even destroying and creating anew.

12. The creation, interpretation, and even administration of normative rules proceed simultaneously with their evaluation. One set of principles by means of which normative rules are created and evaluated is normative principles.

One question that is asked or implied when a normative rule is created or evaluated is: Is the normative rule in accordance with the normative principles believed by the creators and evaluators of it? Hence, when we consider the creation of a normative rule the question "Is it in accord with the principle of justice?" might very well be asked. Or, when it is evaluated, the question might again be asked, "Is it in accord with the principle of justice?" If the answer is affirmative such a rule is called just. And similarly with other normative rules and principles. The connection between normative rules and normative principles is not a logical one, although logic can and should be used to test indirectly the implications of such a connection; and likewise the evaluation of normative rules in terms of 'just' and 'unjust' is ultimately an emotional rather than a logical one.

13. The normative principles of legality and its opposite illegality, equality and its opposite, inequality, equity and its opposite, inequity, and freedom and its opposite, slavery, exhibit the same semantic properties as the principle of justice and its opposite. Hence their detailed treatment will be omitted since it would be analogous to the treatment accorded the principle of justice.

14. We have already indicated that justice cannot be "defined" by fairness and equality. We shall substantiate this further by the following reasoning:

Take as an example the principle of equality before the law. It would be an outright injustice to treat everybody as equal before the law without exceptions and qualifications—children, minors, lunatics, judges, executives, presidents, etc.—and the law indeed does not. Minors, for instance, are not treated as equals with adults before the law because it is felt that they are not responsible for their actions to the same extent as adults. But on the other hand, equality before the law is a normative principle. Thus, to show the absurdity of the matter should one maintain that there is a logical implication between normative principles, we rephrase the case to fit standard logical formulation: equality before the law logically implies justice if and only if equality before the law logically implies injustice.

Moreover, the demonstration that there is no logical connection among normative principles does not imply that there is no emotional connection or accord between them. The emotional accord, however, is no fixed relation, but rather it fluctuates. Hence, it is possible that inequality before the law is accepted as being in accord with the principle of justice at one time and place, whereas at another time and place it is considered not in accord with the principle of justice.

But how is arbitrariness to be avoided if this is so? The only way to avoid arbitrariness at these ultimate sources of law and morality is through the collective experience of mankind. Hence, the progress of the legal and moral consciousness of mankind is the progress in the cultivation and refinement of the emotional feeling for normative principles, or legal and moral culture of mankind. Therefore, incessant efforts and quests of mankind in this direction of progress will never stop, since the cultivation of the emotional feeling for normative principles is a process rather than a finished product. The debate on normative principles will go on and must go on, but it need be neither trivial nor confused. The topics of justice, freedom, equality, legality, and equity are lofty in themselves and so is the emotional feeling for them; none of them need cheap rationalizations to make them respectable in the forum of science.

15. In addition to normative principles there are a number of non-normative principles that are involved in the creation and evaluation of normative rules. They are the principles of effectiveness, realizability, utility, and rationality.

Attempts to use the principle of utility as the sole principle in justifying and evaluating normative rules are responsible to a large extent for the distortions and confusions in theoretical ethics, as are the attempts to exclude it as a principle that somehow vitiates law and morals. And, generally, any monistic approach in ethics that attempts to reduce normative or non-normative principles to a single one will have to end in distortions and confusions for the reason that ultimately it is not the logical relations that prevail among these principles, but the non-logical ones. Hence, as in the case of normative principles, so is it in the case of these non-normative principles; it is impossible to establish the relationship of logical consequence between them. For these principles are also singular terms that cannot subsume other principles or normative rules. But, in contradistinction to normative principles, the construction of their reference is not determined by the emotional feeling but by rational considerations, which can partially be corroborated by experience.

16. The principle of effectiveness was brought to the forefront of juristic discussion by Hans Kelsen. Indeed, the principle of effectiveness represents the criterion for the evaluation of legal systems from the point of view of Kelsen's Pure Theory of Law. But Kelsen's notion of effectiveness differs from ours in that it applies primarily to legal systems and only secondarily to legal rules. Moreover, we extend Kelsen's notion of effectiveness to apply to moral rules as well, and in addition we render it more precise.

17. Let us say that a normative rule is ideally effective exactly when there is no chance that it will ever be violated by anyone under any circumstances; in other words, when the probability of the event that the rule will be complied with is a certainty (i.e., when $P[A] = 1$). Let us also say that a normative rule is ineffective when the chances that it will be complied with are as good as the chances that it will not (i.e., when $P[A] = \frac{1}{2}$). We shall say then that a normative rule is effective when it is neither ineffective nor ideally effective, that is when $\frac{1}{2} < P[A] < 1$. Therefore, to assess whether a normative rule is effective we shall have to determine whether the probability of compliance exceeds $\frac{1}{2}$.

Now historical experience teaches us not only that no normative rule is complied with always and by everyone, but also that some normative rules are complied with more often and by more individuals than others. Also to what extent a normative rule will be complied with depends on the rule itself, the subjects and objects to be controlled by the rule, their social status and the circumstances.

But these details are subject to empirical vicissitudes. Let us introduce, therefore, the distinction of satisfactory and unsatisfactory levels of effectiveness as general theoretical notions and leave the details to descriptive ethics and sociology to determine under which empirical conditions a normative rule will have a satisfactory level of effectiveness and under which it will not.

18. Let a normative system consist of n (n > 1) rules and let m (m < n) be the number of rules of the system that are effective. Further, let k (k < m) be the number of rules of the system that are effective at a satisfactory level. We stipulate now that the normative system be evaluated as effective if and only if the sizes of k and m are satisfactory. But what the satisfactory sizes of k and m are going to be under the given circumstances is no longer a task of theoretical but of descriptive ethics and sociology. However, in general, it can be said that all normative systems have considered k to include the protection of life, person, and property.

19. We introduce the principle of realizability as an empirical criterion of assessment as to whether a contemplated normative rule or system of normative rules is likely to be accepted by the given society and complied with. Hence the principle of realizability is involved in a rational and deliberate creation of normative rules, under the assumption, of course, that the creation of normative rules would be a worthless task if the probability of their realizability were low.

Thus the principles of effectiveness and realizability represent a link between normative rules and normative principles on the one hand, and the social reality and descriptive ethics on the other hand, which is the connection traditionally known under the names of "ought" and "is," and we add also the "can be" in the case of the principle of realizability.

20. The principle of utility was introduced by Beccaria into ethics and popularized by Bentham and his followers. We shall interpret this principle broadly to include public interest and welfare, but, in contra-distinction to the Utilitarians, to exclude the folk-psychological concepts of pain, pleasure, and happiness. The principle of utility can and sometimes does conflict in the process of creation and evaluation of normative rules with the normative principles and even with the principles of effectiveness and realizability.

21. The confusion by Utilitarians of the principle of utility with the folk-psychological concepts of pain, pleasure, and happiness is almost beyond repair. But this is only a part of the story. There is also the occasional Utilitarian application of the principle of utility as if it were a personal tool for evaluating whether a normative rule is "good" or "bad." However, creation and evaluation of normative rules is not a matter for personal decision, but rather social decision. Hence, it is not the "consequences of an action" that are subject to evaluation in terms of the principle of utility, but the intended results of the normative rule. For there is a difference between the consequences of actions performed by individuals and the intended consequences of a normative rule formulated, adjudicated, and administered by the decision-makers of the society.

22. The construction of reference for the singular term 'utility' varies from one social order to another and from one time to another. We may take it that biological survival will be a basic component in the construction of reference for the term 'utility,' which will entail the obtaining of material goods for society at large. But how much beyond biological survival the reference of the term is to include will vary from society to society.

23. The principle of rationality has been used in creating, evaluating, adjudicating, and administering normative rules throughout human history, but it has never been consciously formulated. Yet it is by means of this principle that the conflicts of other principles are composed. Furthermore, intellectual and emotional factors in the life of individuals and societies can be composed in an intelligent way only by an ultimate appeal to the principle of rationality. Hence, the components of the reference of this singular term are in the case of intellectual judgment "good sense," and in the case of emotional feeling "saneness," in individual and collective decisions and assessments.

24. We show now by paradigmatic examples how the principle of rationality can be used to compose conflicts among principles.

Suppose there is an island governed by a small minority of highly skilled and highly sophisticated crooks and thugs. They are exploiters and oppressors of a vast majority. And since no exploitation nor oppression can be carried out on a vast scale and over a period of time without using law for such a purpose, they have created the law and the legal machinery to suit their purpose. Let this law also be effectively administered.

Now, in order to make them violate international law, let this island's government wage an aggressive war against another state, and let them behave in the course of war in a beastly fashion so as to provoke the maximum moral indignation in their enemies. Thereupon let them be defeated and occupied. But let their enemies be fair-minded and sympathetic toward the exploited and oppressed majority. Moreover, let their enemies also be interested in establishing a viable self-government in the island, in order to be able to leave.

The dictates of justice are clear. The guilty ought to be punished and removed from any position of influence and authority. But the dictates of utility are also clear. No matter how great the injustice suffered by those undergoing it, this does not qualify them to run the government and industry. Thus the skilled oppressors are the only ones capable of securing the welfare and even justice in the state, if they can be induced to do so.

What is the occupier to do in such a case? Should he mercilessly chop off heads in the name of justice, or should he keep the thugs in the name of utility? We answer, using the principle of rationality, that the occupier will try to find a solution which will make it possible over a period of time to use the services of thugs while minimizing the potential injustice which they can commit, and in the meantime will try gradually to replace the thugs with skilled and principled members of the oppressed majority.

25. Let us take now a paradigmatic case of a poor fellow with a large family who is assaulted feloniously and permanently disabled. Let the assailants be two men, one of whom is poor and has a large family whereas the other is wealthy, but let all other things be equal. The court pronounces both assailants guilty as charged and proceeds to assess the punishments, which will set the precedent, that is the normative rule which will determine the adjudication of the whole class of similar cases.

The law stipulates that the punishment may include incarceration or monetary indemnification. These are the alternatives: (a) the court may sentence both assailants to equal terms of imprisonment and assess no damages (b) it may sentence both assailants to unequal prison terms and assess no damages; (c) it may sentence both assailants to equal terms and assess equal damages, which becomes meaningless since the poor assailant cannot be forced to pay; (d) it may set equal prison terms for both and assess high damages against the wealthy assailant; (e) it may sentence the assailants to unequal prison terms, the maximum for the poor one and the minimum for the wealthy one, and set the maximum damages against the wealthy one.

Which of these alternatives shall the court choose? These are the principles that the court may use in adjudicating the case: the principles of justice, utility, equality, legality, rationality.

If alternative (a) is chosen the principles of equality and legality, which demand that the assailants be equally treated and punished for the crime will be satisfied, but the principles of justice and utility with respect to the victim and the society, which will have to support him, will be violated.

If alternative (b) is chosen the sentence will satisfy the principle of legality, but violate the principles of equality, justice, and utility.

If alternative (c) is chosen the sentence will satisfy the principle of legality and equality on paper, but not the principle of equality in practice, nor the principles of justice and utility.

If alternative (d) is chosen the sentence will satisfy the principle of legality, justice, and utility, but violate the principle of equality.

Lastly, if alternative (e) is chosen the sentence will satisfy the principles of justice, legality, and utility, but not equality.

The conflict between the principles of justice, equality, legality, and utility will be resolved by means of the principle of rationality, by the fair and wise court, in favor of alternative (e) in this paradigmatic case.

26. The last issue that remains to be raised is the so-called problem of justification.

The problem of justification can be phrased in three questions: (a) How can normative rules be justified? (b) How can normative principles be justified? and (c) How can non-normative principles be justified? The question under (a) can now be answered easily by our theory: Normative rules can be justified by means of ultimate normative and non-normative principles. Questions (b) and (c) can be answered by appeal to intuition and emotional feeling as the ultimate ambiguous sources of normative and non-normative principles, which will necessitate and generate a perennial search into these principles.

THEORY AND PRACTICE IN LAW AND MORALS

I. *The Role of Theory in the Creation and Evaluation of Normative Codes*

1. Normative codes are components of normative orders. Hence, normative theories in a narrower sense are theories of normative codes, but in a broader sense they are theories of normative orders. But, whether normative theories are conceived in a narrower sense, as we have done, or in a broader sense, they must have relevance to normative orders if they are to be realistic.

2. Normative rules are elements of normative codes, which are definable by means of normative rules. Let us say, therefore, that a normative code is a collection of p (p $>$ 1) normative rules. And let us assume that a realizable normative rule has j (j $>$ 1) intended consequences. Normative codes have thus a finite number of normative rules, but are open in the sense that a normative rule can be added to them or canceled out of them at any given moment during their existence as components of normative orders.

3. The notions of effectiveness and realizability of normative rules stipulate that their intended consequences be the control of behavior. Hence, though normative rules may be formed *in abstracto* their intended consequences, the control of behavioral acts, are *in concreto*. And since our stipulation allows for additions and cancellations of normative rules from normative codes, the time element is, as it were, absorbed in our definition. Therefore we can apply our definition at any given time to any code. We illustrate this by an example. Let the normative code have the following three rules:

(1) You shall not kill.
(2) You shall not commit adultery.
(3) You shall not steal.

Thus the code has at the particular moment when the count is taken three rules, each of which has j intended consequences. For example, one of the j intended consequences of rule 3 is the protection of property rights. But this rule can be canceled out, in which case the code will have two rules left.

4. We now stipulate that the creation of normative codes is the process of addition or cancelation of normative rules. Normative codes simply disappear if every rule is canceled out of them, that is, if a point is reached at which $p = o$. Further, since empirical limitations make p finite, a point m (m < p) will be reached when the code will become dead in the sense that it will stop being a component of a normative order. As an example we cite the Code of Hammurabi.

5. Evaluation of normative rules determines the evaluation of normative codes, but only up to a point. Thus if every rule in the code is ineffective or unrealizable, the code is obviously either fictitious or dead. Hence, the code is realistic exactly when there is a number i (i > 1) of rules such that they are either effective or realizable.

We shall say, further, that the code is operational if and only if it is a component of a normative order. Let us assume now that the code is operational. In order to be operational the code must have a certain number i (i > 1) of rules which are effective or realizable. The question now arises, how large must it be in order that the code be operational at a satisfactory level? The answer, however, cannot be given theoretically, since it depends on the given concrete normative and social orders in the sense that they determine how many and which normative rules in the code must be effective or realizable in order that the code be considered at a satisfactory operational level. The determination of the size of it is thus a matter of empirical investigations of normative and social orders.

6. Normative codes can and must be evaluated also in terms of their logical consistency and semantic clarity. This part of the evaluation precedes logically, though not necessarily in time, the previous one; for a code cannot be at a satisfactory level of operation unless it is logically consistent and semantically clear within certain limits of tolerance.

II. *The Role of Theory in Law and Morals*

1. The role of theory in law and morals is initially the same

as in the natural and social sciences: to provide a framework for explanation of empirical phenomena of law and morals. But unlike the theories in natural sciences, the theory of law and morals cannot but have a direct bearing upon the creation of normative phenomena. Thus the decision of the law court to give precedence to one legal rule rather than another in adjudicating a case represents not only an application of legal theory to the rules of the code, but simultaneously the creation of a legal phenomenon, that is, the precedent. The opinions of Roman jurisconsults and Anglo-American judges are classic examples of such a procedure. Hence the theory of law and morals has bearing upon the introduction as well as the cancellation of normative rules. Moreover, it also has bearing upon the introduction and cancellation of normative principles.

2. The theory of law and morals, so far as the explanation of normative phenomena is concerned, can be either adequate or inadequate. It will be adequate if and only if it can satisfactorily explain normative phenomena; otherwise, it will be inadequate.

3. The theory of law and morals, so far as the creation and evaluation of normative phenomena is concerned, will be adequate if and only if it is logically consistent, semantically clear, and relevant to the phenomena of law and morals. The condition of relevance represents the justification, the sole *raison d'être* of the theory.

4. The ordering of human relations is possible only by means of normative rules. But normative rules created in a haphazard fashion, sometimes generated by fanaticism, cannot obtain an order in a highly sophisticated civilization. And this is fundamentally the problem of the twentieth-century world: It has reached the level of civilization where the haphazard creation of normative rules becomes less and less acceptable. Thus an adequate philosophical theory of law and morals becomes a necessity for a rational and just ordering of relations between individuals and groups of individuals.

INDEX